# A Time To Act

# A Time To Act

עת_לעשות

The Report of the
Commission on Jewish Education
in North America

November 1990
Heshvan 5751

Convened by the Mandel Associated
Foundations, JCC Association, and JESNA
in Collaboration with CJF

University Press of America
Lanham•New York•London

University Press of America,® Inc.

4720 Boston Way
Lanham, MD 20706

3 Henrietta Street
London WC2E8LU England

ISBN 0–8191–8104–8 paperback

ISBN 0–8191–8105–6 cloth

# The Commission on Jewish Education in North America

The Commission on Jewish Education in North America was established to launch an unprecedented undertaking — to pool the energies and resources of all sectors of the Jewish community in a mutual effort to enlarge the scope, raise the standards, and improve the quality of Jewish education.

A partnership of the communal and private sectors, the Commission was convened by the Mandel Associated Foundations, the JCC Association, and JESNA in collaboration with CJF. It met six times over a period of two years, from August 1, 1988 to June 12, 1990.

The Commission reflected the diversity of the North American Jewish community and included outstanding community leaders, scholars, educators, rabbis, leaders of the Orthodox, Conservative, Reconstructionist, and Reform denominations, and the heads or the principals of leading foundations.

The idea of forming the Commission was conceived by Morton L. Mandel and his brothers Jack N. Mandel and Joseph C. Mandel of Cleveland, Ohio and financed by the Mandel Associated Foundations.

• • •

*JCC Association*
The Jewish Community Center Association of North America (formerly JWB) is the leadership body for the North American network of JCCs and Ys.

*JESNA*
The Jewish Education Service of North America is the organized community's planning, service, and coordinating agency for Jewish education.

*CJF*
The Council of Jewish Federations is the umbrella organization for Jewish community federations in North America.

## Members of the Commission

### Morton L. Mandel
Chairman

| | | |
|---|---|---|
| Mona Riklis Ackerman | — | President of the Riklis Family Foundation |
| Ronald Appleby | — | Active in Toronto Jewish Congress, Jewish National Fund, Council of Jewish Federations, United Jewish Appeal |
| David Arnow | — | North American Chair, New Israel Fund |
| Mandell L. Berman | — | President, Council of Jewish Federations |
| Jack Bieler | — | Chairman of High School Judaic Studies, Hebrew Academy of Greater Washington |
| Charles R. Bronfman | — | Chairman and Founder, the CRB Foundation |
| John C. Colman | — | President, Jewish Federation of Metropolitan Chicago |
| Maurice S. Corson | — | President, the Wexner Foundation |
| Lester Crown | — | Past Chairman of the Board, the Jewish Theological Seminary of America |
| David Dubin | — | Executive Director, JCC on the Palisades |
| Stuart E. Eizenstat | — | President of the Jewish Community Center of Greater Washington and Honorary Vice-President of the American Jewish Committee |
| Joshua Elkin | — | Headmaster, Solomon Schechter Day School of Greater Boston in Newton |
| Eli N. Evans | — | President, Charles H. Revson Foundation |
| Irwin S. Field | — | Member, Board of Governors, the Jewish Agency for Israel |
| Max M. Fisher | — | Founding Chairman, Board of Governors, the Jewish Agency for Israel |

| | | |
|---|---|---|
| Alfred Gottschalk | — | President, Hebrew Union College-Jewish Institute of Religion |
| Arthur Green | — | President, Reconstructionist Rabbinical College |
| Irving Greenberg | — | President, the National Jewish Center for Learning and Leadership (CLAL) |
| Joseph S. Gruss | — | Founder, Fund for Jewish Education |
| Robert I. Hiller | — | President, the Zanvyl Krieger Fund |
| David Hirschhorn | — | Past Vice-President, American Jewish Committee; active in national and local Jewish communal affairs |
| Carol K. Ingall | — | Executive Director, Bureau of Jewish Education of Rhode Island |
| Ludwig Jesselson | — | Past President and Chairman, UJA/Federation of Jewish Philanthropies of New York Joint Campaign |
| Henry Koschitzky | — | Past Chairman, Board of Jewish Education, Toronto |
| Mark Lainer | — | Vice-President, Jewish Education Service of North America |
| Norman Lamm | — | President, Yeshiva University |
| Sara S. Lee | — | Director, Rhea Hirsch School of Education, Hebrew Union College |
| Seymour Martin Lipset | — | Caroline S.G. Munro Professor of Political Science and Sociology and Senior Fellow, Hoover Institution, Stanford University |
| Haskel Lookstein | — | Principal, Ramaz School; Rabbi, Congregation Kehilath Jeshurun |
| Robert E. Loup | — | Past National Chairman, National Jewish Center for Learning and Leadership (CLAL) |
| Matthew J. Maryles | — | Chairman, Fund for Jewish Education, UJA/Federation of Jewish Philanthropies of New York |
| Florence Melton | — | Founder, the Florence Melton Adult Mini School, the Hebrew University, Jerusalem |
| Donald R. Mintz | — | Honorary President, Jewish Community Centers Association of North America |

| | | |
|---|---|---|
| Lester Pollack | — | President, Jewish Community Centers Association of North America |
| Charles Ratner | — | Chairman, Cleveland Commission on Jewish Continuity |
| Esther Leah Ritz | — | Past President of Jewish Community Centers Association of North America |
| Harriet L. Rosenthal | — | Vice-President, Jewish Community Centers Association of North America |
| Alvin I. Schiff | — | Executive Vice-President, Board of Jewish Education of Greater New York |
| Ismar Schorsch | — | Chancellor and Professor of Jewish History, Jewish Theological Seminary of America |
| Daniel S. Shapiro | — | Past President, Federation of Jewish Philanthropies of New York |
| Margaret W. Tishman | — | Immediate Past President, UJA/Federation of Jewish Philanthropies of New York |
| Isadore Twersky | — | Rabbi, Professor and Director of the Harvard University Center for Jewish Studies |
| Bennett Yanowitz | — | Immediate Past President, Jewish Education Service of North America |

## Commission Staff and Consultants

### Senior Policy Advisors

| | | |
|---|---|---|
| David S. Ariel | — | President, Cleveland College of Jewish Studies |
| Seymour Fox | — | Professor of Education, the Hebrew University, Jerusalem |
| Annette Hochstein | — | Director, Nativ-Policy and Planning Consultants, Jerusalem |
| Stephen H. Hoffman | — | Executive Vice-President, Jewish Community Federation of Cleveland |
| Martin S. Kraar | — | Executive Vice-President, Council of Jewish Federations |
| Arthur J. Naparstek | — | Professor of Social Work, Case Western Reserve University |
| Arthur Rotman | — | Executive Vice-President, JCC Association |
| Carmi Schwartz | — | Executive Vice-President Emeritus, Council of Jewish Federations |
| Herman D. Stein | — | University Professor and Provost Emeritus, Case Western Reserve University |
| Jonathan Woocher | — | Executive Vice-President, JESNA |
| Henry L. Zucker | — | Director, Commission on Jewish Education in North America |

### Director

Henry L. Zucker

### Research and Planning

Seymour Fox, Director
Annette Hochstein, Associate Director

# TABLE OF CONTENTS

# EXECUTIVE SUMMARY

The Jewish community of North America is facing a crisis of major proportions.  Large numbers of Jews have lost interest in Jewish values, ideals, and behavior, and there are many who no longer believe that Judaism has a role to play in their search for personal fulfillment and communality.  This has grave implications, not only for the richness of Jewish life, but for the very continuity of a large segment of the Jewish people.  Over the last several decades, intermarriage between Jews and non-Jews has risen dramatically, and a major proportion of children of such marriages no longer identify themselves as Jews.

It is clear that there is a core of deeply committed Jews whose very way of life ensures meaningful Jewish continuity from generation to generation.  However, there is a much larger segment of the Jewish population which is finding it increasingly difficult to define its future in terms of Jewish values and behavior.  The responsibility for developing Jewish identity and instilling a commitment to Judaism for this population now rests primarily with education.

The Jews of North America have built an extensive and diverse system of education that takes place in many formal and informal settings.  Outstanding educators who are excellent teachers and role models for young people and adults can be found throughout North America in classrooms and community centers, on educational trips to Israel, and in summer camps.  However, the system of Jewish education is plagued by many problems, and because of its inadequacies it is failing to engage the minds of a critical segment of the Jewish population who have no other way of experiencing the beauty and richness of Jewish life.

Careful study of the current state of Jewish education reveals that much of the system, in its various forms and settings, is beset by these problems — sporadic participation; deficiencies in educational content; an underdeveloped profession of Jewish education; inadequate community support; the absence of a research function to monitor results, allocate resources, and plan improvements.

Recent developments throughout the continent indicate that a climate exists today for bringing about major improvements. However, a massive program will have to be undertaken in order to revitalize Jewish education so that it is capable of performing a pivotal role in the meaningful continuity of the Jewish people. It was to achieve this goal that the Commission on Jewish Education in North America was established.

After analyzing the problems, the Commission decided to focus its effort on the two building blocks upon which the entire system rests — developing the profession of Jewish education and mobilizing community support to meet the needs and goals of Jewish education. In order to secure these essential building blocks, a blueprint for the future consisting of a series of concrete steps was worked out by the Commission. The plan includes both short- and long-range elements, and implementation can begin immediately with initial funding already provided.

The core of the Commission's plan is to infuse Jewish education with a new vitality by recruiting large numbers of talented and dedicated educators. These educators need to work in a congenial environment, sustained by a Jewish community that recognizes Jewish education as the most effective means for perpetuating Jewish identity and creating a commitment to Jewish values and behavior.

The plan developed by the Commission includes the following elements:

1. *Building a profession of Jewish education* – By creating a North American infrastructure for recruiting and training increasing numbers of qualified personnel; expanding the faculties and facilities of training institutions; intensifying on-the-job training programs; raising salaries and benefits of educational personnel; developing new career track opportunities; and increasing the empowerment of educators.

2. *Mobilizing community support* – By recruiting top community leaders to the cause of Jewish education; raising Jewish education to the top of the communal agenda; creating a positive environment for effective Jewish education; and providing substantially increased funding from federations, private foundations, and other sources.

3. *Establishing three to five Lead Communities* – To function as local laboratories for Jewish education; to determine the educational practices and policies that work best; to redesign and improve Jewish education through a wide array of intensive programs; to demonstrate what can happen when there is an infusion of outstanding personnel into the educational system, with a high level of community support and with the necessary funding.

4. *Developing a research capability* – By drawing up a comprehensive research agenda for Jewish education; creating the theoretical and practical knowledge base needed to monitor results and make informed decisions; conducting ongoing studies on the state of Jewish education in general, and on the progress of each component of the Commission's plan.

5. *Creating the Council for Initiatives in Jewish Education* – A new entity that will operate as a catalytic agent, working mainly through the efforts of others to ensure the implementation of the Commission's plan; helping to secure necessary funding; overseeing the establishment of Lead Communities; coordinating research activities; providing a setting in which creative people, institutions, organizations, and foundations can work together to develop new undertakings in Jewish education; and helping to replicate the successful experiences in Lead Communities throughout North America.

The Commission is confident that its blueprint is realistic and feasible, and will indeed provide the foundation for a new era in Jewish education. An enormous investment of resources and energies will be required to bring this about, but the Commission is convinced that the will is there and the time to act is now.

# ON THE GOALS OF JEWISH EDUCATION

"Our goal should be to make it possible for every Jewish person, child or adult, to be exposed to the mystery and romance of Jewish history, to the enthralling insights and special sensitivities of Jewish thought, to the sanctity and symbolism of Jewish existence, and to the power and profundity of Jewish faith. As a motto and declaration of hope, we might adapt the dictum that says, 'They searched from Dan to Beer Sheva and did not find an am ha'aretz!' 'Am ha'aretz,' usually understood as an ignoramus, an illiterate, may for our purposes be redefined as one indifferent to Jewish visions and values, untouched by the drama and majesty of Jewish history, unappreciative of the resourcefulness and resilience of the Jewish community, and unconcerned with Jewish destiny. Education, in its broadest sense, will enable young people to confront the secret of Jewish tenacity and existence, the quality of Torah teaching which fascinates and attracts irresistibly. They will then be able, even eager, to find their place in a creative and constructive Jewish community."

*Presented by Professor Isadore Twersky,*
*Member of the Commission,*
*at the meeting of June 12, 1990*

# PREFACE

In August of 1988, the Commission on Jewish Education in North America was convened to initiate a process that could bring about systemic, across-the-board improvement in the quality of Jewish education in the United States and Canada. Our goal was to bring together extensive new resources and energies so that Jewish education could make its fullest contribution to meaningful Jewish continuity.

The composition of the Commission reflected the diversity of the Jewish community and was based on a close partnership between the private and communal sectors. It was comprised of 44 prominent individuals representing key segments of the Jewish community — the heads of institutions of higher learning in the Orthodox, Conservative, Reconstructionist, and Reform movements; educators; rabbis; scholars; heads of foundations; and community leaders.

Never before in North America had such a diverse leadership group come together to address the problems of Jewish education and consider its impact on the Jewish future. Our deliberations over a two-year period and the strategies we have developed demonstrate that enormous power can be marshaled when the different sectors of the Jewish community join forces, develop a consensus, and decide on a plan of action.

Working with the Commission was a group of senior policy advisors consisting of educators, scholars, and the professional heads of major communal organizations. They provided the Commission with valuable experience and expertise in the areas of education, planning, and community organization. Additional counsel was sought from experts in Jewish as well as general education in both North America and Israel. Available data on Jewish education was reviewed, and 11 research papers were especially commissioned to provide a picture of the current state of Jewish education.

The Commission held six plenary sessions between August 1988 and June 1990. A full-time staff prepared background materials for the meetings and maintained continuous written and personal communication with individual commissioners between each of the sessions.

From the outset, all of the commissioners shared the determination to make a concrete impact on Jewish life. We agreed that we would not conclude the work of this Commission without beginning the implementation process the very day we issued our report. We have initiated this process by creating a new entity, the Council for Initiatives in Jewish Education (CIJE), and giving it the mandate to bring about the implementation of our concrete plan of action. Its functions have been set forth in our report, initial funding is already in place, a director has been appointed, and a board of directors is in formation.

The CIJE is now ready to bring our message to the community and launch our plan. It will develop the criteria for Lead Communities and select them; it will immediately help to expand training programs, to recruit capable students for them, and to undertake the complex and sensitive task of introducing large numbers of community leaders to the intricacies of Jewish education.

The CIJE will work in close partnership with CJF, JCC Association, and JESNA. It will also work closely with the institutions and organizations that are delivering the services of Jewish education — the denominations, the Bureaus of Jewish Education, the local federations, the professional organizations, and above all, the front line educators. They have set the groundwork that makes our plan feasible. Over the last few years, through their initiatives and efforts, a climate that is receptive to change and improvement has begun to emerge.

The substantial resources of recently established foundations, a number of which have already given Jewish education a high place on their agendas, will make it possible for ambitious programs to be launched immediately. The foundations represented on this Commission have undertaken pioneering work in the areas of curriculum, adult education, the training of educators, the contribution of Israel to Jewish education, the creative use of the electronic media, and the encouragement of innovation by educators.

I want to thank the members of the Commission for giving so generously of their time and wisdom, and for their willingness to rise above real and legitimate differences of viewpoint in order to agree upon this ambitious, yet realistic plan of action.

With the issuance of this report, the Commision on Jewish Education in North America has achieved its primary objective. Ahead lies the challenge of implementation and the

opportunity to make a significant difference. We are deter-
mined to face squarely the problems of our educational system
and to help usher in a new era in Jewish education.

> Morton L. Mandel
> Chairman
> The Commission on
> Jewish Education
> in North America

# CHAPTER ONE

# FACING THE CRISIS

*There is a* deep and widespread concern in the Jewish community today that the commitment to basic Jewish values, ideals, and behavior may be diminishing at an alarming rate. A substantial number of Jews no longer seem to believe that Judaism has a role to play in their search for personal fulfillment and communality. This has grave implications not only for the richness of Jewish life but for the very continuity of a large segment of the Jewish people.

Throughout history Jews have faced dangers from without with courage and steadfastness; now a new kind of commitment is required. The Jews of North America live in an open society that presents an unprecedented range of opportunities and choices. This extraordinary environment confronts us with what is proving to be an historic dilemma: while we cherish our freedom as individuals to explore new horizons, we recognize that this very freedom poses a dramatic challenge to the future of the Jewish way of life. The Jewish community must meet the challenge at a time when young people are not sure of their roots in the past or of their identity in the future. There is an urgent need to explore all possible ways to ensure that Jews maintain and strengthen the commitments that are central to Judaism.

In our uniquely pluralistic society, where there are so many philosophies and ideologies competing for attention, and where the pursuit of Judaism increasingly involves a conscious choice, the burden of preparation for such a decision resides with education. Jewish education must be compelling — emotionally, intellectually, and spiritually — so that Jews, young and old, will say to themselves: "I have decided to remain engaged, to continue to investigate and grapple with these ideas, and to choose an appropriate Jewish way of life." Jewish education must be sustained, expanded, and vastly improved if it is to achieve this objective. It must become an experience that inspires greater numbers of Jews to learn, feel, and act in a way that reflects a deep understanding of Jewish values.

### A System Under Strain

The difficulties facing Jewish education bear some resemblance to the problems of education in general in North America. Well-known reports have documented the serious shortage of teaching talent and a slackening of academic standards. A severe lack of funds, resources, status, and vision is causing the system to strain and crack. Jewish education is equally impoverished in regard to these basic requirements.

There are exceptions. Some in the community have maintained an intensive, vibrant educational system for all age groups. This includes yeshivot, day schools, and extensive courses for adult learning.

However, this system — often highly traditional — serves but a small proportion of the Jewish population, while for the vast majority in North America today, Jewish education is frequently limited in scope. At times it is confined simply to teaching facts about Jewish history and holidays and some study of the Hebrew language. Many additional elements that should be central to the mission of Jewish education — such as Jewish values and ideals, the attachment to the State of Israel and concern about Jews throughout the world, the meaning of prayer, the relationship with God and community — are often lacking. It is imperative that at this moment in history, Jewish education become a formative rather than merely an informative experience. Without such change, it will be increasingly difficult to pass on to future generations a strong identity with and commitment to Judaism.

Jewish education must find a way to transmit the essence of what Jewish life is all about, so that future generations of Jews will be impelled to search for meaning through their own rich traditions and institutions. Judaism must be presented as a living entity which gives the Jews of today the resources to find answers to the fundamental questions of life as readily as it did for our ancestors through the centuries. Otherwise it could eventually be overtaken in the minds of many people by other systems of thought they feel are more meaningful for the modern world.

## Competing Demands

This dangerous state of affairs is in no small measure the result of the historical, social, and cultural factors that have affected the priorities of the Jewish community. While there has always been support for Jewish education from the religious denominations (the Orthodox, the Conservative, and the Reform), and while many outstanding schools, community centers, and summer camps have been established, the leaders of the organized Jewish community have focused their attention on other serious issues.

At the turn of the century, the chief emphasis was on financial support for the indigent newcomers and on their Americanization. In the '20s and '30s, the Jewish community focused on providing health and social services and on dealing with problems of anti-Semitism. During the post-war period, the highest priority was given to the life-saving work of Jewish relief, rehabilitation, and reconstruction, and to building the State of Israel. Subsequently, the development of communal services in North America and the security and growth of the State of Israel became the primary concern. Currently, the Jewish community is mobilized for the rescue and resettlement of Soviet Jewry.

In the face of such life-and-death issues, the needs of education have seemed to be less urgent, less insistent, more diffused; a problem that could be dealt with at some point in the future when more pressing problems have been solved. This is an illusion. We may continue to live with emergencies indefinitely, but we can no longer postpone addressing the needs of Jewish education, lest we face an irreversible decline in the vitality of the Jewish people.

The attitudes of the Jewish community have also been influenced over the years by the desire of many to become fully integrated into American society, and by the belief that an intensive Jewish education was not consistent with the achievement of this goal. One of the correlates of this outlook is the rise in intermarriage and the turning away from Jewish traditions in the search for fulfillment and meaning in life. According to a recent Gallup (Israel) Poll of American Jews, conducted in December 1989, the number of intermarriages has sharply increased in the past couple of decades. Currently, 28% of Jews under the age of 40, more than one in four, are intermarried, compared with 16% of Jews between the ages of 40 and 59. These figures are consistent with studies of individual communities in North America undertaken in recent years.

*A Weakening Commitment to Jewish Life*

Research data indicate that Jews who intermarry are significantly less likely to provide their children with a Jewish education and that these children are far less likely to identify themselves as Jews.

Another symptom of the problem is that while a large majority of Jewish children have at one time or another received some form of Jewish education, it has often been so sporadic that it has had little impact on their lives. A recent study found that over half of Jewish school age children in the United States are not currently enrolled in any kind of Jewish schooling. Inevitably, children with little or no Jewish schooling will grow up with a relatively weak identification with and understanding of Judaism, and have difficulty passing on to their children an appreciation of the beauty and richness of Jewish life.

In the past, the Jewish family and the Jewish community had certain bonds that gave them remarkable inner strength. Jews grew up in families and neighborhoods with a strong Jewish ambiance. They were constantly surrounded by the symbols and customs of Jewish life. They came into contact with their cultural and spiritual heritage in a variety of institutions and settings. Thus young people received a strong sense of Jewish identity through experiences in their everyday life. Today there are few such neighborhoods, and the way of life they represented has all but disappeared, as has the lifestyle that brought ongoing contact and interrelationship with grandparents and extended family members.

There is also reason to be concerned that the attachment to Israel, which is essential to the identity of so many Jews, is decreasing. This is particularly so for those who were born after the Holocaust and the establishment of the State of Israel.

The weakening commitment to Jewish life, which can already be seen in the lives of the current generation of young adult Jews, may become even more apparent among their children and grandchildren. This painful prospect, which community leaders can foresee in their own families as well as in the community at large, has brought to a head concern about the quality and mission of Jewish education.

It was to meet this challenge that the idea of creating the Commission on Jewish Education in North America was born.

# CHAPTER TWO

# THE REALITIES OF JEWISH EDUCATION TODAY

*he underlying assumption* that guided the Commission was that the North American Jewish community had the capacity to mobilize itself for education as it had in the past for the building of the State of Israel, the rescue of Jews in distress, and the fight against discrimination. This would require that all sectors of North American Jewry join forces, pool their energies and resources, and launch an unprecedented undertaking to enlarge the scope, raise the standards, and improve the quality of Jewish education. To accomplish this, the Commission decided to review the current state of Jewish education in its various aspects. This would provide the basis for analyzing the problems, considering the achievements and shortcomings, and determining where the most promising opportunities for improvement might lie.

## The Diversity of the Field

It is clear that Jewish education today encompasses a broad range of learning experiences. Hundreds of thousands of American

Jews of all ages are currently involved in one way or another in education in formal and informal settings. A multitude of institutions offer a wide variety of educational activities. Many of these institutions are under the auspices of individual religious denominations — the Orthodox, the Conservative, the Reconstructionist, the Reform. Others are part of communal or independent organizations. Altogether they include day schools, yeshivot, supplementary schools, synagogue-based programs of study and informal activities, community centers, programs at colleges and universities, youth movements, summer camps, educational visits to Israel, early childhood programs, adult and family programs, retreat centers, and museums. Thousands of educators — some estimates say 30,000 — staff these institutions and activities. (See Table 1.)

In addition, there are many other ways in which Jewish content is communicated to the Jews of North America — through the print and broadcast media, cultural events, films, books, and lectures. All of these combined contribute to the diversity and richness of the field of Jewish education. It is estimated that more than $1 billion is spent annually on Jewish education.

### *Shortcomings in Specific Settings*

Despite the extensive range of activities, Jewish education is not achieving its mission. Exposure to existing Jewish educational programs leaves many North American Jews indifferent to Judaism, and unwilling or unable to take an active part in Jewish communal living.

## TABLE 1: THE FACTS AND FIGURES OF JEWISH EDUCATION*

JEWISH POPULATION

|  | UNITED STATES (1987) | CANADA (1989) |
|---|---|---|
| TOTAL | 5,944,000 | 310,000 |
| SCHOOL AGE (AGES 3–17) | 880–950,000 | 57,000 |

1. *Day Schools* — 800 schools; 120,000 participants

2. *Supplementary Schools* — 1,700 schools; 280,000 participants

3. *Jewish Community Centers* — 220 centers and branches; close to one million members, many more occasional participants in activities

4. *Camping* — 12,000 children in day camps; 85,000 children in residential camps

5. *Youth Movements* — 75,000 members; another 25,000 occasional participants

6. *Educational Visits to Israel* — 25,000 participants in a large variety of programs

7. *Early Childhood Programs* — 50,000 participants

8. *Adult Education* — 5–10% of the adult population participate in formal and informal programs

9. *Retreat or Conference Centers* — In 50 cities in North America

10. *Family Education* — Several hundred family programs ranging from one–time activities to family camps or year–long courses

11. *College–age Program* — Over 600 colleges and universities offer courses and academic programs in Judaica. About 100,000 students are served by Jewish agencies on campus.

12. *Training Istitutions for Educators* — 14 training institutions in North America. 358 students currently enrolled for BA's and MA's. 100 graduates annually. Training also takes place in Israel, particularly for senior educators.

*The data in this report represent a compilation of sources reflecting current available statistics on Jewish education in North America as well as research undertaken for the Commission. Sources are listed in Appendix D.

Why is this happening?

Although all of these institutions and areas of activities offer great promise for Jewish education, each is plagued by serious problems.

Supplementary schools, for instance, have for years reached the largest number of Jewish children in the United States. Yet they continue to face difficulties in motivating students who have spent a full day at public school, who have ongoing homework responsibilities, and who have a variety of competing interests such as television, sports, music, and other leisure-time activities. Although there are notable exceptions, over the past several decades there has been a significant decline in the role and quality of such schools. As one commissioner put it, "As long as supplementary school is something you have to live through rather than enjoy, it cannot be valuable. So many Jewish-Americans have had an impoverished supplementary school experience as their only Jewish education."

Day schools have been increasing in number and size of student body; however, they still only reach 12% of the total Jewish student population. At present, the vast majority of Jewish parents choose not to enroll their children in a school environment they perceive as confining. Moreover, policy makers question the prospects of continued growth in light of the high cost of tuition, which is prohibitive even for many middle-class families. At the same time, for many schools there is a severe shortage of qualified teachers and curricular materials.

Jewish Community Centers are engaged in a major effort to make Jewish education a central element in their programming;

the challenge facing them is how to convert this institution into a major force for Jewish education within a framework that is primarily recreational, social, and cultural.

Early childhood programs under Jewish auspices have been growing in number because increasingly both parents work. However, many of these programs have not made Jewish education their primary focus because of a severe shortage of trained personnel.

Jewish education programs on college campuses could potentially reach a large portion of the estimated 400,000 Jewish students who attend colleges and universities. Yet at the present time, they reach no more than 25% of this audience. On most campuses, the impact of these programs is limited.

It is well known that Israel speaks powerfully to its visitors, but it is extremely underutilized as a resource for Jewish education. The majority of American Jews have never been to the country, and many Jewish educators have not availed themselves of Israel's educational resources, which are large in number and diverse in nature.

Both family and adult education are growing in importance and participation; however, at present there is an insufficient body of knowledge about how to make these programs work. For the most part, they involve infrequent meetings and suffer from a dearth of appropriate educational materials.

Youth movements, which at one time were powerful feeders for community leadership and Jewish professional life, have lost a good deal of their vigor and are suffering from a declining membership.

Although there have been some remarkable success stories in Jewish summer camps, such camps tend to be expensive, and many do not have Jewish education as a central purpose.

Finally, there is no question that the print and broadcast media, and innovative forms of learning through the use of computers, museum exhibitions, films, and videocassettes, offer tremendous opportunities for the future of Jewish education. But this is still a virtually untapped field, and only a few quality programs have been created.

### Overall Problems

In addition to the shortcomings specific to each area of Jewish education, there are serious overall problems that affect the field. Sporadic participation, deficiencies in educational content, inadequate community support, an underdeveloped profession of Jewish education, and a lack of reliable data — these problems manifest themselves in many of the settings, forms, and age groups.

### Sporadic Participation

Jewish education is a voluntary system. This means that unlike the obligation for continuing participation that is accepted in general education for given age groups, in Jewish education attendance is discretionary. With so many diversions and competing interests at work in North American society today, sustained involvement can only be achieved when there is genuine engagement and commitment. The lack of such involvement has resulted in a general pattern of sporadic participation for many types of Jewish educational activities. This state of affairs is in conflict with the fundamental commitment that Judaism requires for lifelong learning.

There are close to one million Jewish children of school age in North America. Most of these children, perhaps as many as 80%, have attended some form of Jewish schooling at least one time in their lives. However, for many, attendance is often short-lived and sporadic. Close to 600,000 children currently do not receive any form of Jewish schooling. Only some 400,000 in the U.S. (about 40% of all Jewish children), and 32,000 in Canada (about 55%) are currently enrolled in any Jewish school. The problem is more pronounced with children over Bar Mitzvah, Bat Mitzvah, or Confirmation age, when attendance drops by more than 60%. (See Figure 1.)

Over a 20-year period, from 1962 to 1982, total enrollment in Jewish schools in the U.S. declined by nearly 35%. It is esti-

FIGURE 1:  AVERAGE ENROLLMENT IN SUPPLEMENTARY SCHOOL
PER AGE AND GRADE LEVEL (U.S., 1982/3)

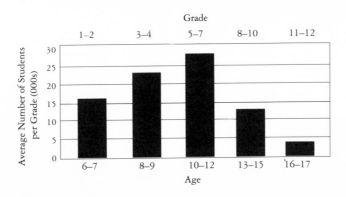

■ Supplementary Schools

Source: Dubb and DellaPergola (1986)

mated that about half of this decline reflects a lessening interest in Jewish schooling, the other half negative demographic trends (the end of the baby boom). It is interesting to note that during this time period the most extensive form of Jewish education in the U.S., the supplementary school, declined by about 50%, from 540,000 to 280,000, while day school enrollment rose from 60,000 to 110,000, a rise of 80%. (See Figure 2.) However, even for day school, attendance falls off sharply after elementary school.

### FIGURE 2: ENROLLMENT U.S.: 1962 & 1982

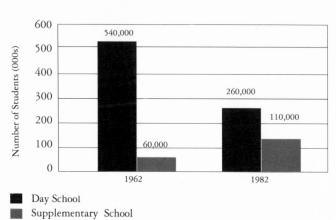

Based on Dubb and DellaPergola (1986)

Part of the difficulty encountered in Jewish schools, particularly the supplementary school, is the discrepancy between what takes place in the school setting and the environment at home. If there is insufficient appreciation or respect for Jewish values and traditions in the home environment, it stands to reason that children will not be motivated to participate seriously and continuously in Jewish schooling.

A study based on direct observation of supplementary schools reveals a clear connection between a child's home life and the effectiveness of Jewish education. According to David Schoem in "Explaining Jewish Student Failure" (1982):

> "...the explanation for failure of students in the Jewish school lay in their parents' and their own perception that there was no compelling reward to be expected from their education... The 12-year-olds who complained that 'Hebrew school doesn't matter' were speaking truthfully about the attitudes and behavior they saw valued at home and in the community... For them, going to Harvard 'counted'; studying a portion of the Torah did not."

Studies show that participation in Jewish learning continues to drop as Jews enter adulthood. Among college-age students, no more than an estimated 25% avail themselves of Jewish education services. And only one in ten Jewish adults continues to be involved in any type of organized Jewish learning.

### Deficiencies in Educational Content

Much of the subject matter presented in Jewish education fails to inspire students. One reason is that Jewish education has not yet had the benefit of enough thinking and planning in the areas of educational content and curriculum development.

Although general education is beset by many problems in this regard, it invests substantial resources in centers that specialize in such areas as science education, the teaching of the humanities and social sciences, and the development of methods of language instruction. Very little of a comparable nature is being done in the field of Jewish education.

For example, there are few centers that specialize in deveoping effective methods for teaching the Hebrew language, Jewish history, and the great Jewish texts — the Bible, the Talmud, and the key philosophical writings from the medieval period to the present day. Very few teachers have been encouraged to specialize and take leadership in any of these areas. Nor have they been supported in their efforts to create educational materials for Jewish schools and informal education. Consequently, there is a dearth of appropriate curricular and educational materials for early childhood education, the day and supplementary schools, informal education, and adult education.

As a result of this deficiency, the vast majority of Jews are not adequately exposed to the great ideas of the Jewish tradition. And without such knowledge and experience it is virtually impossible to develop a deep and lasting commitment to Jewish learning.

### Inadequate Community Support

The Jewish community has not yet recognized the indispensable role it must play in order for Jewish education to achieve its goal. Community leaders have often failed to make the connection between the educational process and the knowledge that leads to commitment.

It is this lack of understanding that has prevented the top community leadership in North America from rallying to the cause of Jewish education in the same way it has to other pressing needs of the Jewish people. The constituencies of most national and local organizations have not yet recognized that

Jewish education is indispensable to their futures.

As a result, the environment in the Jewish community is not sufficiently supportive of the massive investment required to bring about systemic change. This affects the priority given to Jewish education, the status of the field of Jewish education, and the level of funding that is granted.

Inevitably, insufficient community support limits the aspirations, inhibits the vision, and stifles the creativity of those involved in all aspects of Jewish education.

### The Underdeveloped Profession of Jewish Education

There is a severe shortage of talented, trained, and committed personnel for the field of Jewish education. It is estimated that there are some 30,000 positions for Jewish education in North America, of which about 5,000 are full-time. Many positions in the school system are unfilled every year when school opens in September. Yet only 101 students graduated in 1989 from all Jewish education training programs. (This does not include programs under Haredi auspices.) The vast majority of the available teaching positions will be filled by individuals who have not been trained as Jewish educators.

Most of those who enter the field do so with far less education than their counterparts in the public education system. Thus, while over half of public school teachers hold a Master's Degree, this is true of only a small percentage of teachers in Jewish day schools. Fewer than half of the teachers in the supplementary schools have had a high school Jewish education. Informal educators are trained in various disciplines but receive almost no pre-service training in Jewish education. In-service education is not compulsory or systematic. Thus, front-line educators are not kept informed of advances and developments in the practice and theory of Jewish education.

One reason for the difficulty in attracting serious professionals to the field is the part-time nature of many of the teaching positions. Of the total number of Jewish school teachers, it is estimated that only about 15% to 20% hold full-time positions. Isa Aron and Bruce Phillips have reported in "Findings of the Los Angeles Bureau of Jewish Education Teachers Census" that only 23% of all the teachers in Los Angeles teach more than 20 hours per week, while 54% teach under 10 hours.

Low salaries, a serious problem in general education, are even more prevalent in Jewish education. Only 14% of Jewish educators in Los Angeles earn $20,000 or more, while 41% — part-time teachers — earn under $3,000 a year. Only 20% receive health benefits. In 1988, supplementary school teachers carrying a 12-hour work load per week earned an average annual salary of $9,000. Early childhood teachers earned an average of $10,000. Full-time day school teachers carrying a 30-hour teaching load per week earned an average annual salary of $19,000. These figures are lower than the average public school teacher's salary of $25,000 for kindergarten teachers and $30,000 for elementary school teachers (according to the latest National Education Association figures), which in itself is recognized as woefully inadequate.

Moreover, throughout the United States, supplementary Jewish education experiences a high rate of teacher turnover. According to the Report on Jewish Continuity of the Jewish Community Federation of Cleveland, there was an annual teacher turnover rate in Cleveland schools of approximately 20% in 1986. Other communities around the country have reported a similar pattern.

Another problem is that often the best teachers in the schools find themselves promoted to the role of school principals. The ladder of advancement in Jewish education is essentially linear — from teacher to assistant principal to principal. There is almost no opportunity for advancement other than administrative; it is difficult for talented teachers to assume leadership roles and specialize in the teaching of such subjects as Hebrew, the Bible, Jewish history, or in the fields of early childhood, family education, and special education. This is yet another deterrent for many individuals who might otherwise enter the field: it limits both the professional and intellectual growth of teachers.

Few Jews today are choosing Jewish education as a career, and this will leave the next generation of young Jews educationally impoverished unless something is done to reverse this trend. Aryeh Davidson, in "The Preparation of Jewish Educators in North America," reports that teaching faculty at the training institutes are also in short supply. This year, all training programs together have only 18 full-time faculty who specialize in Jewish education. It is obvious that so small a faculty cannot possibly undertake the many assignments that the training institutions must fill.

As one considers these problems, it becomes obvious that the salaries, training, working conditions, and status of Jewish educators have an important bearing on the problems of recruitment and retention of qualified personnel for the field of Jewish education. For Jewish education to become an attractive profession, it will have to develop clearly defined standards, appropriate terms of employment, a high level of training, and a network of collegial support.

### The Lack of Reliable Data

Very little research on Jewish education is being carried out in North America. There is a paucity of data about the basic issues, and almost no evaluation has been made to assess the quality and impact of programs.

Because of this, decisions are taken without the benefit of clear evidence of need, and major resources are invested without sufficient monitoring. We do not know what people want to learn, and we seldom know what works in Jewish education. We do not even know much about what students know at different stages of their education. There are not enough standardized achievement tests. There is not sufficiently accurate information on the number of teachers in the system, their qualifications, and their salaries.

We also need more extensive investigation into the history and philosophy of Jewish education in order to enrich the creative process that will help design the Jewish education of tomorrow.

### Prospects for the Future

The review of the field of Jewish education presents a disturbing but not necessarily discouraging picture. When faced with the realities of Jewish education today, the commissioners recognized that while there are great shortcomings that need to be overcome, there are also significant examples of outstanding successes in every one of the settings in which Jewish education takes place. Thus, there are a number of day schools and supplementary schools in which students are able to develop a deep understanding of Jewish life. There are a number of community centers that provide meaningful Jewish experiences to their members. There are a number of summer camps in which young people learn to translate Jewish principles and ideas into everyday living. And there are a number of organized educational visits to Israel that convey an appreciation of the extraordinary rebirth of a nation and of the renaissance of the Hebrew language.

Above all the commissioners were mindful that there are many dedicated and inspiring educators who succeed in engaging the minds of their students and in helping them find their way within the Jewish tradition.

The challenge facing the Commission was to study the conditions that would make it possible for such successful programs to be replicated and for outstanding educators to serve as models for the entire field.

The commissioners recognized that this could only be accomplished if the enormous problems that beset the field were faced squarely. Only then could a plan be developed that would enable Jewish education to achieve its mission and become a more powerful force in contemporary Jewish life.

# CHAPTER THREE

# THE BUILDING—BLOCKS OF JEWISH EDUCATION

*T*here are so many aspects of Jewish education which urgently need attention that it was difficult for the commissioners to decide where to begin. Several issues needed to be resolved for the Commission's plan of action: What area of education should provide the focus for the Commission's work? What implementation strategy would be most likely to succeed? Should work begin locally or continentally? Who would implement the plan?

### Focusing the Work of the Commission

Commissioners identified 23 specific areas of education, each of which would be important enough in itself to warrant the attention of a special commission. (See Table 2.) The question was how to select those that would have the most significant impact and be most likely to effect substantial change in the field of Jewish education. The 23 areas were analyzed in terms of this question.

## Table 2: Areas Suggested for the Commission's Agenda

1. The early childhood age group
2. The elementary school age group
3. The high school age group
4. The college age group
5. Young adults
6. The family
7. Adults
8. The retired and the elderly
9. The supplementary school
10. The day school
11. Informal education
12. Israel experience programs
13. Integrated programs of formal and informal education
14. The Hebrew language, with special initial emphasis on the leadership of the Jewish community
15. Curriculum and methods
16. The use of the media and technology (computers, videos, etc.) for Jewish education
17. The shortage of qualified personnel for Jewish education
18. The Community – its leadership and its structures – as major agents for change in any area
19. Assistance with tuition
20. The physical plant (buildings, laboratories, gymnasia)
21. A knowledge base for Jewish education (research of various kinds: evaluations and impact studies, assessment of needs, client surveys, etc.)
22. Innovation in Jewish education
23. Additional funding for Jewish education

Clearly, it would not make sense for the commissioners to concentrate on a particular educational setting, since each of these touch only a segment of the Jewish population. Similarly, the commissioners were reluctant to focus on a specific age group, since all ages are important. Attention was particularly drawn to the five overall problems that affect the system — sporadic participation, deficiencies in educational content, an underdeveloped profession of Jewish education, inadequate community support, and the lack of reliable data.

Upon analysis, it became clear that the most fundamental problems facing Jewish education are an underdeveloped profession of Jewish education and inadequate community support.

There is a shortage of well-trained and dedicated educators for every area of Jewish education. They are needed in order to motivate and engage children and their parents, to create the necessary educational materials and methods, and to design and carry out a wide variety of research studies.

However, only if there is a fundamental change in the nature of community support for Jewish education is it likely that large numbers of talented young people will be attracted to careers in Jewish education. Only if community leaders will give Jewish education the high priority it deserves on the local and national agenda will the resources necessary for a program of major improvement be obtained. Only if the climate in the community is supportive of Jewish education will qualified teaching personnel be attracted to its new career opportunities.

Here then was the key to developing a comprehensive plan.

The Commission's work would focus on these two necessary conditions for change and improvement:

- Personnel — developing a profession of Jewish education
- The community —recruiting leadership, securing funding, and developing appropriate structures.

Because these two areas have implications for all of the others, they can be considered the "building blocks" of Jewish education, upon which major improvement of the entire Jewish educational system rests.

### Developing a Comprehensive Approach

There have been noteworthy attempts in the past to deal with the serious shortage of qualified educational personnel. Efforts have been made to raise salaries and to recruit students for training programs; however, dealing with single elements has not met with success. Indeed, talented people will not be recruited to training programs unless these lead to attractive positions. Reasonable salaries will not solve the problem of retention unless there are prospects for advancement and growth.

In fact, the commissioners came to the conclusion that any plan would have to be comprehensive and devoted simultaneously to recruiting and training large numbers of qualified educators as well as to building career opportunities and offering reasonable salaries and benefits. The Commission's plan would not meet with success if it addressed only one of these elements; they must be addressed simultaneously.

The commissioners also realized that personnel and the community were interrelated, each being dependent on the other for success. For Jewish education to attract talented and dedicated Jews to the field, these individuals must believe that the Jewish community will give them the resources necessary to make the difference.

At the same time the community will only be mobilized for the cause of Jewish education if it believes that a highly qualified profession of Jewish educators is being developed.

As work with the "building blocks" proceeds, it will provide the foundation for improvements in programmatic areas — schools, JCCs, summer camps, Israel experience programs, curriculum development, and the sophisticated use of the electronic media. With large numbers of talented and well-trained educators entering the field, new and creative approaches in these areas will be developed.

### Short-Range and Long-Range Strategies

Because of the vast scope of the field of Jewish education (30,000 educators, thousands of educational institutions) it would be difficult to bring about across-the-board changes throughout North America within a short time period. Moreover, education takes place locally, in communities and in institutions. Thus both a short-range and long-range strategy would need to be developed and they would include both local and continental components.

The short-range plan would concentrate on creating local models through which the Jewish community could learn what works best in Jewish education. It would demonstrate in a small group of communities what could happen if sufficient numbers of outstanding personnel are recruited and trained, if their efforts are supported by the community and its leadership, and if the necessary funds are secured to maintain such an effort over a period of several years.

The long-range plan would focus on establishing a North American infrastructure for recruiting and training increasing numbers of qualified personnel. This would involve working with training institutions to expand their faculties and facilities, to develop innovative training programs, and to establish extensive in–service education programs.

The plan would also call for a major effort in the community to take the steps that would raise Jewish education to the top of the communal agenda and create a better environment — a better climate — for Jewish education.

*Implementing the Plan*

The core of the Commission's plan would be to infuse Jewish education with a new vitality by recruiting and training large numbers of talented and dedicated educators. These educators need to work in a congenial environment, sustained by a Jewish community that recognizes Jewish education as the most effective means for perpetuating Jewish identity and creating a commitment to Jewish values and behavior.

To accomplish this objective, an entity would have to be created to ensure the enactment of the many phases of the Commission's plan. A research capability would also have to be established to provide reliable data on work being done and monitor the impact of various activities.

The ultimate goal would be to bring about across-the-board improvement in as many aspects of Jewish education as possible for all segments of the Jewish community.

# CHAPTER FOUR

# A BLUEPRINT FOR THE FUTURE

*A* *series of concrete* steps were worked out by the Commission as a blueprint to achieve the objectives of its overall plan. These steps would assure that the plan would be more than a list of worthy goals; that it would also set in motion a process that could bring about tangible results over a period of time.

The plan includes the following elements:

I.    BUILDING A PROFESSION OF JEWISH EDUCATION
II.   MOBILIZING COMMUNITY SUPPORT
III.  ESTABLISHING LEAD COMMUNITIES
IV.   DEVELOPING A RESEARCH CAPABILITY
V.    CREATING THE COUNCIL FOR INITIATIVES IN JEWISH EDUCATION

### I. BUILDING A PROFESSION OF JEWISH EDUCATION

Profession building, as envisioned by the commissioners, will be accomplished by creating a North American infrastructure for recruiting and training increasing numbers of qualified personnel; expanding the faculties and facilities of training institutions; intensifying in–service education programs; raising salaries and benefits of educational personnel; developing new career track opportunities; and increasing the empowerment of educators. Specifically, the following concrete measures have been offered for consideration:

*Recruitment*

A marketing study will be conducted to identify those segments of the Jewish population in which there are potential candidates for careers in Jewish education, and to determine what motivations or incentives would be most likely to attract gifted people to the field. Thus, for instance, while it is obvious that equitable salary levels are an important motivating factor, there is some evidence that empowering educators to have an increased impact on the lives of students is even more significant.

The marketing study will help determine how to reach the key target groups for recruitment — graduates of day schools, students participating in Jewish camps, college students studying in Judaica departments, students participating in Israel experience programs, and professionals at mid-career who are looking to make career changes.

Based on the results of the marketing study, a recruitment plan will be undertaken. This may involve visits by educational consultants and trained recruiters to the major colleges and universities that have large Jewish populations. It may also include visits to Jewish summer camps, consultations with participants in work/study programs in Israel, and meetings with participants in community center activities.

An important part of the recruitment plan will be spreading

the word through articles, speeches, seminars, and other forms of communications that Jewish education is about to undergo a major transformation. These efforts could help stimulate the interest of potential candidates in key target groups. Promotional materials (newsletters, brochures, videos, etc.) may be produced to maintain a constant flow of information to these groups, thereby creating an awareness of the exciting changes that are taking place in the field.

### Developing New Sources of Personnel

Jewish education must build upon the nascent idealism of many young people and attract them to the profession. There is a reservoir of young Jews who are outstanding academics and professionals in the humanities and social sciences who would welcome the opportunity to make a contribution to Jewish life for a few years. Such individuals could be recruited as Fellows of Jewish Education, bringing their expertise to the field of Jewish education in areas such as curriculum, teaching methods, and the media. They will serve as consultants to educators and educational institutions, and will help monitor and evaluate specific programs.

Another source of talent could be outstanding college students who are specializing in Judaica at colleges and universities, or are graduates of day schools and of Hebrew speaking camps. Although they may be heading for careers in law, medicine, or business and are not planning a lifelong career in education, many such students would be attracted to the idea of joining a Jewish Education Corps. This will involve spending several years of service in the Jewish educational system — as teachers in supplementary or day schools and as educators in community centers and other informal programs. The Jewish Education Corps would be similar in some respects to the Peace Corps. Agreements will be made in which these young people commit themselves to a fixed number of teaching hours a week for a set number of years. They will undergo special training and agree to pursue studies in Judaica during this time period, while also continuing their general studies. In exchange for their teaching services, they will receive appropriate remuneration.

Fast-Track Programs will be created for young men and women majoring in Judaica at colleges and universities who are attracted to the new opportunities in Jewish education. Because of their knowledge of Jewish subjects, they can be prepared in a relatively short period of time to assume important educational positions. It is estimated that there are hundreds of potential candidates for such positions who are currently studying Judaica subjects. Unlike the Jewish Education Corps, Fast-Track Programs will prepare students to enter full-time careers in Jewish education. They will steer students toward some of the prime educational positions that will be created as a result of the Commission's plan.

Career-Changers are also a promising source of new personnel for Jewish education. These are individuals in their thirties and forties who are interested in making major career changes to find more personally satisfying and more emotionally rewarding work. People from the corporate world, the legal profession, the arts, and other fields are turning to general education as a way to make a serious impact on the next generation. Those with good Jewish backgrounds represent an important potential for Jewish education. They bring with them a degree of maturity and life experience that can be extremely valuable.

Such individuals will be recruited for Jewish education as part of the Commission's program.

### Training

The Commission's plan calls for an expansion of training opportunities in North America and in Israel. Student bodies and faculties of current training institutions will be enlarged; new training programs for specialized fields and subjects will be developed; leadership training programs will be established; in-service education for practicing educators will be intensified; and the important contribution of Israel to each one of these areas will be expanded. To accomplish this, substantial funding will be sought for program development, for additional faculty positions, and for student fellowships. One foundation participating in the Commission's work has already made significant grants to help initiate such efforts.

The immediate target is to increase the number of graduates of the training institutions from the current level of 100 annually to at least 400. Thus over a 10-year period, significant progress could be made in filling the estimated 5,000 full-time positions in the Jewish educational system with well-trained personnel.

This expansion will require the enlargement of the full-time educational faculty in training institutions. New faculty positions could be filled by recruiting outstanding practitioners in the field, scholars from yeshivot, and academics from universities. Specialized programs will be created to prepare educators for new positions in such fields as informal education, early childhood education, family education, and the teaching of Bible, history, Hebrew, and other subjects.

A cadre of leaders will be prepared to assume key positions in Jewish education — professors of Jewish education, researchers, curriculum developers, teacher trainers, directors of bureaus, heads of community centers, and principals for model and experimental schools. Promising candidates will be recruited at mid-career to participate in tailor-made programs. Other programs will be developed in North America, similar to the Jerusalem Fellows in Israel and the Senior Educators at the Hebrew University in Jerusalem, which have succeeded in recruiting, training, and placing more than 100 educators in leading positions throughout the world.

In-service education will be expanded through courses, seminars, and conferences organized by continental and local service agencies, by the training institutions, as well as by departments of Judaica at various general universities in North America and in Israel. CAJE and other professional organizations will be encouraged to enlarge their contribution to on-the-job training. Financial assistance will be provided to individuals in the Jewish educational system in order to make it possible for them to participate in these new programs. In time, this should become standard practice and basic to the professional growth of all of those who are working in formal and informal education.

## Improvement of Salaries and Benefits

Salaries and benefits for educational personnel must be substantially increased in order to be competitive with other fields attracting talented Jews today. Unless this problem is addressed, it will be difficult to convince our most gifted young people to devote their lives to Jewish education. A determination will be made as to appropriate remuneration levels necessary to retain dedicated and experienced educators, and funds will be raised to cover the additional costs.

The role of federations in this area will be crucial. Once standards are developed for different salary levels and benefits, local federations will be encouraged to incorporate these in their fundraising targets and allocations. There are a number of communities and institutions which have already taken steps in this direction and can provide helpful models for this process. Public reports will be issued periodically on the progress being made in regard to increasing salary and benefits in Jewish education throughout North America.

## Career Track Development

A career development program for educators will be created to provide for professional advancement. Front line educators such as teachers will be offered a variety of career path options. At present, the only path of advancement open to teachers is linear — from teacher to assistant principal to principal. Such new options will make it possible for teachers to assume leadership roles without having to move into administration. An expert in early childhood education or in teaching the Bible or Hebrew can make as important a contribution to Jewish education as the principal of a school. Appropriate positions will be created to enable such experts to play a larger role in the school system and thus have influence beyond his or her classroom.

### The Empowerment of Educators

Gifted educators need to be empowered to have an influence on curriculum, teaching methods, and the educational philosophy of the institutions in which they work. Active programs will be undertaken with the institutions and agencies involved in Jewish education to develop ways of granting educators the opportunity to be involved in the decision-making process and play a meaningful role in the administration of schools and community centers.

This will require a reorientation of educational policy. Schools will be encouraged to develop incentives for teachers who show special promise in this regard. New positions with appropriate status will be developed for those who have the desire and ability to contribute significantly to the educational direction of their schools. Progress is already being made along these lines: one family foundation involved in the work of the Commission has already developed a program that will provide awards to creative educators who have developed outstanding programs.

Each of these elements will contribute significantly to building a profession of Jewish education. Talented people will be attracted to the profession when they believe they can make a difference and are given the means and resources to do so. This means being empowered to help shape the content and methods in their own institutions, receiving adequate salaries and benefits, and being recognized as playing a leading role in determining the future of the Jewish people.

## II: Mobilizing Community Support

A number of strategies will be developed to increase community support for Jewish education. Their aims are to recruit top community leaders to the cause of Jewish education; raise Jewish education to the top of the communal agenda; create a positive environment for Jewish education; and provide substantially increased funding from federations, private family foundations, and other sources.

### Recruiting Community Leaders

Top community leaders will be recruited individually to the cause of Jewish education by members of the Commission and other influential personalities who are able to convey the urgency of providing support for Jewish education. The North American Jewish community has demonstrated an unusual capacity to deal with major problems when they are addressed by the very top community leaders.

Efforts will be made to involve lay leaders who are members of the boards of Jewish schools, synagogues, and JCCs in the

Commission's plan. Members of local federations will be made aware of the steps that have to be taken in their local communities in order to improve Jewish education.

The goal is clear. As one commissioner observed, a majority of community leaders must rally to the cause of Jewish education. "The chances are," he said, "that in 1980, only a few of these leaders thought Jewish education was a burning issue, many thought it was important, and the rest didn't spend much time thinking about it. In 1990, it may well be that there are significantly more community leaders who think that education is a burning issue, more who think it is important, and fewer who don't give it too much attention. The challenge is that by the year 2000, the vast majority of these community leaders should see Jewish education as a burning issue and the rest should at least think it is important. When this is achieved," the commissioner concluded, "money will be available to finance fully the massive program envisioned by the Commission."

### Increased Funding for Jewish Education

The revitalization of Jewish education will require a substantial increase in funding — to raise teachers' salaries, pensions, and other benefits, to provide new positions, to increase the faculty of training institutions, to provide fellowships for students, and to develop new training programs and expand in-service education.

Long-term support for Jewish education will be provided by current sources — tuition income, congregational and organizational budgets, and fundraising, as well as by gradually increasing federation allocations. An exciting new development that holds great promise for the field is the serious entry of strong private foundations into Jewish education. This is unprecedented. A number of foundations, some represented on the Commission, have decided to invest substantial sums in Jewish education and indeed have already begun to do so. Some will support specific elements of the Commission's action plan. Also, many federations have a relatively new resource available through successful endowment programs and are in a promising position to help give a quick start to new and innovative programs.

*Changing the Community's Attitude toward Jewish Education*

The very creation of the Commission on Jewish Education in North America in 1988 — which brought together for the first time scholars, community leaders, educators, heads of foundations, and the leaders of the Orthodox, Conservative, Reconstructionist, and Reform movements — signaled the readiness of the Jewish community to join together in a massive effort to improve Jewish education. Over a two-year period, its deliberations have themselves helped to create a climate in which major change can take place.

A potential base of larger support in communities in North America is also evidenced by a number of local commissions on Jewish education/continuity that have been established in the past few years (there are already more than 10 such commissions). The important work being done by the JCC Association through its Commission on Maximizing the Jewish Educational Effectiveness of Jewish Community Centers demonstrates the results that can be achieved when community support is galvanized. The regional conferences recently organized by JESNA — which will culminate in a continental conference — are heightening community awareness of the crucial significance of Jewish education to meaningful Jewish continuity.

The Commission report and follow-up plans will inform all segments of the Jewish community that Jewish education will be undergoing a period of genuine revitalization. It will be given widespread distribution so that Jewish leadership throughout the country will be aware that this plan is not just another symbolic gesture or limited endeavor, but is the initiation of a broadscale effort. The report will be made available to members of the boards of congregations and schools, and to leaders of all Jewish religious, educational, social, and communal organizations.

As the plan developed by the Commission gets under way, a continuing flow of information will keep community leaders apprised of the progress being made. Communications through all appropriate channels will be sustained in the months and years ahead concerning the implementation of the programs.

Seminars and conferences will be organized for community leaders to acquaint them with the many different aspects of the plan that are being carried out. It will be important for them to be aware of the role they can play in helping to build a profession of Jewish education.

The Commission has decided to continue its work, although in a modified format. Its members will be convened by the Council for Initiatives in Jewish Education (CIJE) and will meet once a year. At that time an update will be issued to inform the Jewish community on the progress of its plan. These reports will also be distributed to important sectors of the Jewish community.

## III: Establishing Lead Communities

Many of the activities described above for the building of a profession of Jewish educators and the development of community support will take place on a continental level. However, the plan also calls for intensified local efforts.

### *Local Laboratories for Jewish Education*

Three to five model communities will be established to demonstrate what can happen when there is an infusion of outstanding personnel into the educational system, when the importance of Jewish education is recognized by the community and its leadership, and when the necessary funds are secured to meet additional costs.

These models, called "Lead Communities," will provide a leadership function for other communities throughout North America. Their purpose is to serve as laboratories in which to discover the educational practices and policies that work best. They will function as the testing places for "best practices" — exemplary or excellent programs — in all fields of Jewish education.

Each of the Lead Communities will engage in the process of redesigning and improving the delivery of Jewish education through a wide array of intensive programs.

## Selection of Lead Communities

Fundamental to the success of the Lead Communities will be the commitment of the community and its key stakeholders to this endeavor. The community must be willing to set high educational standards, raise additional funding for education, involve all or most of its educational institutions in the program, and thereby become a model for the rest of the country. Because the initiative will come from the community itself, this will be a "bottom-up" rather than a "top-down" effort.

A number of cities have already expressed their interest, and these and other cities will be considered. The goal will be to choose those that provide the strongest prospects for success. An analysis will be made of the different communities that have offered to participate in the program, and criteria will be developed for the selection of the sites.

Once the Lead Communities are selected, a public announcement will be made so that the Jewish community as a whole will know the program is under way.

## Getting Started

Lead Communities may initiate their programs by creating a local planning committee consisting of the leaders of the organized Jewish community, rabbis, educators, and lay leaders in all the organizations involved in Jewish education. They would prepare a report on the state of Jewish education in their community. Based on their findings, a plan of action would be developed that addresses the specific educational needs of the community, including recommendations for new programs.

An inventory of best educational practices in North America would be prepared as a guide to Lead Communities (and eventually made available to the Jewish community as a whole). Each local school, community center, summer camp, youth program, and Israel experience program in the Lead Communities would be encouraged to select elements from this inventory. After deciding which of the best practices they might adopt, the community would develop the appropriate training program so that these could be introduced into the relevant institutions. An important function of the local planning group would be to monitor and evaluate these innovations and to study their impact.

The Lead Communities will be a major testing ground for the new sources of personnel that will be developed. They will be a prime target for those participating in the Fellows program as well as the Jewish Education Corps. In fact, while other communities around the country will reap the benefits of these programs, the positive effects will be most apparent in the Lead Communities.

The injection of new personnel into a Lead Community will be made for several purposes: to introduce new programs; to offer new services, such as adult and family education; and to provide experts in areas such as the teaching of Hebrew, the Bible, and Jewish history.

Thus Lead Communities will serve as pilot programs for continental efforts in the areas of recruitment, the improvement of salaries and benefits, the development of ladders of advancement, and generally in the building of a profession.

## IV. Developing a Research Capability

A research capability for Jewish education in North America will be developed at universities, by professional research organizations, as well as by individual scholars. They will create the theoretical and practical knowledge base that is indispensable for change and improvement. A comprehensive, long-range research agenda will be outlined. It will involve the creation of settings where scholars and practitioners can think together systematically about the goals, the content, and the methods of Jewish education. It will include procedures for the evaluation of each component of the Commission's plan and the gathering of new information concerning the state of Jewish education generally.

The research results will be disseminated throughout the Jewish community for use in short-term and long-term planning. Data on Lead Communities will be analyzed to ensure that their individual programs are educationally sound and are meeting with success.

## V: ESTABLISHING THE COUNCIL FOR INITIATIVES IN JEWISH EDUCATION

A new entity, the Council for Initiatives in Jewish Education, will be created to see to it that the plan of the Commission is implemented, both on continental and local levels.

The Council will be a significant enterprise but modest in size organizationally. It will not be a direct service provider. Rather it will operate as a catalytic agent, working through the efforts of others — JESNA, JCC Association, CJF, the institutions of higher Jewish learning, the denominational departments of education, CAJE, and other professional educational organizations. No existing organization plays this role today in Jewish education.

To carry out its mission, the Council will be a strong advocate on behalf of Jewish education. It will develop comprehensive planning programs and experimental initiatives for the two building blocks — personnel and community — to achieve breakthroughs in Jewish education. It will designate the Lead Communities and work with them to initiate their programs. It will stimulate the development of a research capability for Jewish education in North America. It will also provide a setting in which creative people in institutions, organizations, and foundations can work together to develop new undertakings in Jewish education.

The Council will be an independent body. Its Board of Directors will be drawn from among the leaders of the foundation community, continental lay leaders, outstanding Jewish educators, and leading Jewish scholars. The initial annual operating budget of the Council will cover the cost of staff and facilities to carry out its work.

*Spreading the Word: The Diffusion of Innovation*

Another major function of the Council will be to set up a process whereby communities around the country will be able to learn, adapt, and replicate the ideas, findings, and results of the Lead Communities. In this phase of the Council's work, continental organizations — especially JESNA, JCC Association, CJF, and the denominations — will play a critical role, since they will provide the means by which this process can be effected.

The Council will encourage these organizations to develop procedures that will accomplish this objective through published reports, seminars, editorial coverage in the Jewish and general media, on-site visits to Lead Communities by community leaders and educators, and eventually through training programs for community leaders around the country.

As Lead Community programs begin to bear fruit, plans will be developed by the Council to establish new Lead Communities. At the end of the first five years, it is expected that the initial Lead Communities will have matured and developed a momentum of their own towards a continually improving educational system. By that time, another three or four Lead Communities may be added to the plan. These communities will be able to move forward at a more rapid pace, based on what is learned in the first communities.

The process of adding new communities should be a continuing one, so that in time there will be a growing network of active participants in the program. It also may be possible to establish a new category of Lead Communities that will function as associates of the original communities. This program will thus have a ripple effect and, as time goes on, be extended into an increasing number of communities throughout North America.

# CHAPTER FIVE

# A TIME TO ACT

*D*uring *the two-year* process of working out the details of a blueprint for the future, an underlying question surfaced from time to time as to whether, in the present environment, even the most successful achievement in Jewish education could make a fundamental difference in the outlook of a new generation of Jews.

It was clear that there continues to be a core of deeply committed Jews whose very way of life ensures meaningful Jewish continuity from generation to generation. However, the thrust of the Commission's thinking was directed at the much larger segment of the Jewish population which is finding it increasingly difficult to define its future in terms of Jewish values and behavior.

The commissioners realized that there was no way to guarantee that education is going to resolve this issue for the majority of Jews today. But it is also clear that education is the only means by which this goal can be achieved. The same is true in other fields of human endeavor. Thus, while there is no guarantee that the medical profession will find the cure to all diseases, we know that without effective hospitals, well-trained doctors, and systematic medical research, it is not possible to achieve any progress in health care. Similarly, without effective education-

al institutions, outstanding educators, and the meaningful pre-
sentation of the great ideas of the Jewish tradition, it will not be
possible to bring about a deepening involvement of Jews with
Judaism.

Perhaps the most important question the Commission faced
was: How seriously can the Jewish community in North America be committed at this time to such a mission? The commissioners were confident that the blueprint they developed was
realistic and could, indeed, provide the foundation for a new
era in Jewish education. However, results could only be achieved
if there was the will and determination to make an enormous
investment of resources and energies in the decades ahead. At the
conclusion of their deliberations, the commissioners were convinced that the will is there and that the time to act is now.

As the commissioners evolved their plan for the future, they
became increasingly hopeful that a wide range of educational
possibilities would arise once the building blocks were firmly
established. They foresaw a time when the field would attract
some of the most creative Jewish minds of our era, bringing
entirely new approaches to education.

One dramatic opportunity for future development discussed
during the Commission's meetings is in the area of telecom-
munications. The success of recent television programs of Jewish content on both public and commercial networks is a clear
indication of the vast potential of this new field. The explo-
sion of cable television suggests that one day it may be possible
with the flick of a dial to tune in to programs of Jewish dance,
music, drama, interviews with Jewish writers and political fig-

ures, and to receive daily programs from Israel. Indeed a new "electronic village," as described by one commissioner, could in the near future enable Jews of all ages to interact with many aspects of their Jewish heritage on a continuing basis.

Many other technological developments — the use of computers, video disk technology, multi-media exhibitions — could provide a framework in which great educators can communicate with vast audiences. This would be particularly significant in regard to that segment of the Jewish population which is not involved in organized Jewish life.

Equally impressive developments may take place in other programmatic areas as the Commission plan gets under way. The infusion of educational institutions such as schools and community centers with new energy, the introduction of new programs for family and adult education, and the expansion of educational programs in other institutions such as museums and libraries will open up new vistas for Jewish education.

The timeliness of this whole endeavor was dramatized by the great upheavals that are taking place on the world stage and in Jewish life — communist dictatorships are being supplanted in Eastern Europe, the U.S. and the U.S.S.R. are moving towards a reduction of armaments and tensions, a great exodus is taking place of Jews from the Soviet Union to Israel.

The Commission's work was not occasioned by any of these historic developments, nor was it immune to their impact. They gave even greater weight to its purpose, for it is the values and learning central to Jewish education that bind our people together around the globe, and make us sensitive to the repercussions of external events.

Ultimately, the Commission recognized as it completed its work that the measure of its achievement would be the degree to which its program would enable contemporary Jews to fulfill the biblical injunction:

> "And these words, which I command thee this day, shall be upon thine heart; and thou shalt teach them diligently unto thy children, and shalt talk of them when thou sittest in thine house, and when thou walkest by the way, and when thou liest down, and when thou risest up."

(Deuteronomy 6:4-9)

# ACKNOWLEDGEMENTS

The Commision was fortunate to have as its director Henry L. Zucker, one of the most distinguished and experienced Jewish communal professionals in North America. Mr. Zucker guided the work of the Commission with great sensitivity to the commissioners and to the pluralism they represented. His extensive knowledge and experience were invaluable for the work of the Commission.

The enormous contributions of Professor Seymour Fox of the Hebrew University, Jerusalem, who served as chief education advisor, and of Annette Hochstein, director of Nativ–Consultants, Jerusalem, who was responsible for research and planning, is particularly noteworthy. Many indivisuals contributed to the work of the Commission, but none on such a large scale and in such an inspired way.

Our senior policy advisors maintained regular contact with commissioners and extended and enriched the deliberations far beyond the six Commission meetings. They made themselves available for innumerable meetings and consultations and were generous in sharing their wisdom and experience.

Professor Michael Inbar of the Hebrew University, Jerusalem, served as consultant for research and methodology. His ideas were important in shaping the direction of the Commission's work. The Commision was able to recruit a group of distinguished researchers who undertook and successfully completed a complex assignment in a very limited amount of time. The staff of JESNA, JCC Association, and CJF shared important data and information with Commission staff and advisors on a regular basis. CAJE, the largest organization of Jewish educators, convened a group of experts from among its members to advise the Commission on important educational issues.

Virginia Levi carried the major responsibility for organizing and coordinating the entire endeavor. She administered the work of the Commission ably and almost single–handedly. Mark Gurvis and Professor Joseph Reimer facilitated the research program and served as liaison with the many organizations that worked with the Commission. In Jerusalem, Debbie Meline and Estelle Albeg provided essential research, and editorial and administrative assistance.

David Finn, our editor, fulfilled the complex assignment of communicating the message of the Commission to the community at large. He and his associate Dena Merriam, of Ruder•Finn, Inc., brought many significant insights to the preparation of this report.

As the Commission concluded its work, it was able to recruit Stephen H. Hoffman, executive vice–president of the Jewish Community Federation of Cleveland, as director of the Council for Initiatives in Jewish Education. He has assumed the leadership role in transitioning from the work of the Commission to the implementation of the plan.

## APPENDIX A:

### Members of the Commission on Jewish Education in North America

*Mona Riklis Ackerman* (Ph.D.), New York, NY — Dr. Ackerman is a clinical psychologist and President of the Riklis Family Foundation. She is active in UJA/Federation of Jewish Philanthropies of New York and American Friends of Rechov Sumsum.

*Ronald Appleby* (Q.C.), Toronto, Ontario — Mr. Appleby is Chairman of the law firm of Robins, Appleby & Taub, involved mainly in business income tax consultations; he speaks and writes regularly on this subject. He is active in many civic and Jewish causes, including the Toronto Jewish Congress, Jewish National Fund, Council of Jewish Federations, and United Jewish Appeal.

*David Arnow* (Ph.D.), New York, NY — Dr. Arnow is a psychologist, North American Chair of the New Israel Fund, and Chair of the UJA/Federation of Jewish Philanthropies of New York Subcommittee on Governance.

*Mandel L. Berman,* Southfield, MI — Mr. Berman is formerly President of Dreyfus Development, a real estate development company. He is immediate past Chairman of the Skillman Foundation, President of the Council of Jewish Federations, and a past President of the Detroit Federation. He served as Chairman of the American Association of Jewish Education and is Honorary Chairman of JESNA. He is a member of the Board of the Dreyfus Corporation.

*Jack Bieler* (Rabbi), Silver Spring, MD — Rabbi Bieler is Coordinator of High School Judaic Studies and Lead Teacher at the Hebrew Academy of Greater Washington. He has served as Chairman of the Talmud Department at the Joseph H. Lookstein Upper School of Ramaz, Permanent Scholar-in-Residence of Congregation Kehilath Jeshurun, and is a Jerusalem Fellow.

*Charles R. Bronfman,* Montreal, Quebec — Mr. Bronfman is Co-Chairman and Chairman of the Executive Committee of the Seagram Company, Ltd., Chairman of the CRB Foundation, President of UIA Canada, and Honorary Chairman of Canada-Israel Securities, Ltd. He is active in many other civic and Jewish causes.

*John C. Colman,* Glencoe, IL — Mr. Colman is a private investor and business consultant. He is a member of the Executive Committee of the American Jewish Joint Distribution Committee, President of the Jewish Federation of Metropolitan Chicago, Chairman of the Center for Social Policy Studies in Israel, and is active in a wide variety of Jewish and general institutions.

*Maurice S. Corson* (Rabbi, D.D.), Columbus, OH — Rabbi Corson is President of the Wexner Foundation. He was a Director of the Jewish Community Relations Council of Philadelphia, Executive Director of the United Israel Appeal of Canada, and Associate Director of Development for B'nai B'rith International. He is active in many Jewish and civic causes. Prior to entering the field of communal service, Rabbi Corson served as a congregational rabbi in Baltimore, Maryland; Ventnor, New Jersey; and Seattle, Washington.

*Lester Crown,* Chicago, IL — Mr. Crown is President of Henry Crown and Company, Chairman of the Board of Material Service Corporation, and Executive Vice-President of General Dynamics. He has served as Chairman of the Board of the Jewish Theological Seminary of America.

*David Dubin,* Tenafly, NJ — Mr. Dubin is Executive Director of the Jewish Community Center on the Palisades and author of several articles in "The Journal of Jewish Communal Service" on Jewish education within Jewish community centers.

*Stuart E. Eizenstat,* Washington, D.C. — Mr. Eizenstat practices law in Washington, D.C. and teaches at the Kennedy School of Government at Harvard University. He was Director of the Domestic Policy Staff at the White House under the Carter Administration. He is President of the Jewish Community Center of Greater Washington and Honorary Vice President of the American Jewish Committee.

*Joshua Elkin* (Rabbi, Ed.D.), Newton, MA — Rabbi Elkin is Headmaster of the Solomon Schechter Day School of Greater Boston, Newton, Massachusetts. He has taught in the Jewish Education concentration of the Hornstein Program in Jewish Communal Service at Brandeis University and is a Jerusalem Fellow.

*Eli N. Evans,* New York, NY — Mr. Evans is President of the Charles H. Revson Foundation which supports programs in urban affairs, Jewish and general education, and biomedical research policy. He has written two books on the history of Jews in the American South.

*Irwin S. Field,* Cerritos, CA — Mr. Field is President of Liberty Vegetable Oil, and Director of Luz International, Ltd. He is a Member of the Board of Governors — Jewish Agency for Israel, Vice Chairman of the Jewish Federation of Los Angeles, past National Chairman of the United Jewish Appeal, and a trustee of Occidental College. He serves many other national and international organizations.

*Max M. Fisher,* Detroit, MI — Mr. Fisher is founding Chairman of the

Board of Governors of the Jewish Agency for Israel, President of the Council of Jewish Federations, and President of the United Jewish Appeal. He was Chairman of United Brands Company and has been involved with many other corporations and civic and Jewish organizations.

*Alfred Gottschalk* (Rabbi, Ph.D.), Cincinnati, OH — Dr. Gottschalk is President of the Hebrew Union College-Jewish Institute of Religion and Professor of Bible and Jewish Religious Thought. He is founder of the School of Jewish Communal Service and Chairman of the Academic Committee of the U.S. Holocaust Memorial Council. He also serves as Vice-President of the World Union for Progressive Judaism. He has written extensively on education and Jewish intellectual history.

*Arthur Green* (Rabbi, Ph.D.), Wyncote, PA — Dr. Green is President of the Reconstructionist Rabbinical College and the author of many books and articles, including *Tormented Master: A Life of Rabbi Nahman of Bratslav.*

*Irving Greenberg* (Rabbi, Ph.D.), New York, NY — Rabbi Greenberg is President and co-founder of CLAL: the National Jewish Center for Learning and Leadership. He founded and chaired the Department of Judaic Studies at City College. He has taught and written widely on Jewish thought and religion and is author of *The Jewish Way* (1988).

*Joseph S. Gruss,* New York, NY — Mr. Gruss is former head of Gruss & Company. He established the Fund for Jewish Education in New York in association with UJA/Federation of Jewish Philanthropies. He has provided full medical and financial support to Jewish educators, grants to 400 Jewish Day Schools and Yeshivot and to community organizations dedicated to Jewish outreach, and funds for school building renovations. He supports Jewish educators through scholarships for high school and college students.

*Robert I. Hiller,* Baltimore, MD — Mr. Hiller is a consultant to nonprofit organizations and President of the Zanvyl Krieger Fund. He has been Chief Professional Officer of the Council of Jewish Federations and the Jewish Federations in Pittsburgh and Baltimore.

*David Hirschhorn,* Baltimore, MD — Mr. Hirschhorn is Vice-Chairman of American Trading and Production Corporation. He is past Vice-President of the American Jewish Committee. He is also active in national and local Jewish communal affairs, including the Associated (Federation), Baltimore, Sinai Hospital, and the Institute of Christian-Jewish Studies.

*Carol K. Ingall,* Providence, RI — Mrs. Ingall is Executive Director of the Bureau of Jewish Education of Rhode Island and curriculum consultant to the Melton Research Center of the Jewish Theological Seminary of America.

*Ludwig Jesselson,* New York, NY — Mr. Jesselson has served as Chairman of Philipp Brothers, Inc., is Chairman of the Board of Governors of Bar Ilan University, past President and Chairman, UJA/Federation of Jewish Philanthropies of New York Joint Campaign, and is Chairman of the Board of Yeshiva University.

*Henry Koschitzky,* Toronto, Ontario — Mr. Koschitzky, a former Rhodes Scholar, is President of Iko Industries, Ltd. He has served as Chairman of the Board of Jewish Education in Toronto.

*Mark Lainer,* Encino, CA — Mr. Lainer is an attorney and real estate developer. He is an officer of the Jewish Federation of Los Angeles and Vice-President of JESNA. He was founding President of Abraham Joshua Heschel Day School, Vice-President of Education at Temple Valley Beth Sholom, Encino, and Chairman of the Bureau of Jewish Education of Los Angeles.

*Norman Lamm* (Rabbi, Ph.D.), New York, NY — Dr. Lamm is President of Yeshiva University, founder of Tradition magazine, and the author of many books, including *Torah Umadda: The Encounter of Religious Learning and Worldly Knowledge in the Jewish Tradition.* He was a member of the President's Commission on the Holocaust and lectures extensively on Judaism, law, and ethics.

*Sara S. Lee,* Los Angeles, CA — Mrs. Lee is Director of the Rhea Hirsch School of Education at Hebrew Union College in Los Angeles and President of the Association of Institutions of Higher Learning in Jewish Education. She is a frequent contributor to conferences and publications on Jewish education.

*Seymour Martin Lipset* (Ph.D.), Stanford, CA — Professor Lipset is the Caroline S.G. Munro Professor of Political Science and Sociology and Senior Fellow at the Hoover Institution at Stanford University. He has been co-editor of "Public Opinion" and author of many books, including *Political Man* and *The Politics of Unreason.*

*Haskel Lookstein* (Rabbi, Ph.D.), New York, NY — Rabbi Lookstein is Principal of Ramaz School and Rabbi of Congregation Kehilath Jeshurun. He teaches at Yeshiva University and has served in leadership roles with the National Rabbinic Cabinet of UJA, the New York Board of Rabbis, the Coalition to Free Soviet Jews, and the UJA/Federation of Jewish Philanthropies of New York.

*Robert E. Loup,* Denver, CO — Mr. Loup is a real estate developer. He is life President of the Allied Jewish Federation of Denver, past National Chairman of CLAL, a member of the Board of Governors of the Jewish Agency, and past National Chairman of the United Jewish Appeal.

*Morton L. Mandel,* Cleveland, OH — Mr. Mandel is Chairman of the Board of Premier Industrial Corporation, Cleveland, Ohio, and founded and chaired the Commission on Jewish Education in North America. He served as Chair of the Jewish Education Committee of the Jewish Agency, and was President of the Council of Jewish Federations and the JCC Association (formerly JWB). He is founding Chair of the World Confederation of Jewish Community Centers.

*Matthew J. Maryles,* New York, NY — Mr. Maryles is a Managing Director of Oppenheimer & Company, Inc., a New York investment banking firm. He is former President of Yeshiva of Flatbush, Chairman of the Fund for Jewish Education, and an active Board Member of UJA/Federation of Jewish Philanthropies of New York.

*Florence Melton,* Columbus, OH — Mrs. Melton is the founder of the Florence Melton Adult Mini School, a community-based, two-year formal school for serious adult learners. The curriculum was developed at the Hebrew University in Jerusalem. Through her philanthropic efforts, she has initiated numerous innovative projects in Jewish and general education. Mrs. Melton is the founder of the R.G. Barry Corporation, where she serves as Consultant for development and design. She has served on the Board of Huntington National Bank, Columbus, and is an inventor who holds a number of patents.

*Donald R. Mintz,* New Orleans, LA — Mr. Mintz is a senior partner of Sessions & Fishman and a Professor at Tulane University Law School. He was President of the Jewish Federation of Greater New Orleans and is Honorary President of Jewish Community Centers Association of North America (formerly JWB).

*Lester Pollack,* New York, NY — Mr. Pollack is a General Partner of Lazard Freres & Company, Chief Executive Officer of Centre Partners, and Senior Managing Director of Corporate Partners. He is President of the JCC Association and Vice-President of UJA/Federation of Jewish Philanthropies of New York.

*Charles Ratner,* Cleveland, OH — Mr. Ratner is Executive Vice-President of Forest City Enterprises, Inc. He is Vice-President of the Jewish Community Federation of Cleveland, Chairman of the Cleveland Commission on Jewish Continuity, and Chairman of the Cleveland Jewish Welfare Fund campaign. He is also active in other civic and Jewish organizations.

*Esther Leah Ritz,* Milwaukee, WI — Mrs. Ritz has been President of the JCC Association and Vice-President of the Council of Jewish Federations. She is past President of the Milwaukee Jewish Federation and has served on the boards of the Shalom Hartman Institute, JDC, HIAS, UJA, CLAL, and the Wurzweiler School of Social Work.

*Harriet L. Rosenthal,* South Orange, NJ — Mrs. Rosenthal is a Vice-President of the JCC Association. She was a delegate of the National Council of Jewish Women to the Conference of Presidents and serves on the Board of the National Conference on Soviet Jewry.

*Alvin I. Schiff* (Ph.D.), New York, NY — Dr. Schiff is Executive Vice-President of the Board of Jewish Education of Greater New York, a much-published author, editor of Jewish Education, former Professor of Jewish Education and head of the Graduate Department of Education at Yeshiva University, and past President of the Council for Jewish Education.

*Ismar Schorsch* (Rabbi, Ph.D.), New York, NY — Dr. Schorsch is Chancellor and Professor of Jewish History at the Jewish Theological Seminary of America. He has served as President of the Leo Baeck Institute and has published in the area of European Jewish history.

*Daniel S. Shapiro,* New York, NY — Mr. Shapiro is a partner in Schulte, Roth & Zabel. He has served as President of the Federation of Jewish Philanthropies of New York and Vice-President of the Council of Jewish Federations.

*Margaret W. Tishman,* New York, NY — Mrs. Tishman was the first President of the Combined UJA/Federation of Jewish Philanthropies of New York from 1986-89. She has served in leadership roles with the Jewish Community Relations Council of New York, the Jewish Theological Seminary, Yeshiva University, and the Jewish Home and Hospital for the Aged. She is a past President of the Central Bureau for the Jewish Agency. She is a Director of the Jewish Agency for Israel, the American Jewish Joint Distribution Committee and the Hebrew Immigrant Aid Society.

*Isadore Twersky* (Rabbi, Ph.D.), Cambridge, MA — Professor Twersky is Nathan Littauer Professor of Hebrew Literature and Philosophy and Director of the Center for Jewish Studies at Harvard University. Author of numerous scholarly books and studies in Jewish philosophy and law, he is also Rabbi of the Talner Bet Midrash in Brookline, Massachusetts.

*Bennett Yanowitz,* Cleveland, OH — Mr. Yanowitz is a principal in the firm of Kahn, Kleinman, Yanowitz, and Arnson. He is immediate past President of Jewish Education Service of North America (JESNA). He has served as Vice-President of the Jewish Community Federation of Cleveland and Chairman of the National Jewish Community Relations Advisory Council.

## APPENDIX B:

### Staff and Consultants to the Commission on Jewish Education in North America

#### SENIOR POLICY ADVISORS

*David Ariel* — President and Associate Professor at the Cleveland College of Jewish Studies. Has taught at Wesleyan University and is the author of a book on Jewish mysticism.

*Seymour Fox* — Professor of Education and Chairman of the Academic Board of the Samuel Mendel Melton Centre for Jewish Education in the Diaspora at the Hebrew University of Jerusalem. Academic Director of the Jerusalem Fellows.

*Annette Hochstein* — Director, Nativ-Policy and Planning Consultants, Jerusalem, Israel; Humphrey Fellow in Public Policy at MIT, 1983-84.

*Stephen H. Hoffman* — Executive Vice-President of the Jewish Community Federation of Cleveland.

*Martin S. Kraar* — Executive Vice-President of the Council of Jewish Federations (CJF) since November 1989. Previously served as Executive Vice-President of the Jewish Welfare Federation of Detroit, Vice-President of the Jewish Federation of St. Louis, and Director General of the CJF Israel Office.

*Arthur J. Naparstek* — Former Dean and currently Professor of Social Work, Mandel School of Applied Social Sciences, Case Western Reserve University.

*Arthur Rotman* — Executive Vice-President, Jewish Community Centers Association of North America (JCC Association) and President, World Conference of Jewish Communal Service.

*Carmi Schwartz* — Former Executive Vice-President, Council of Jewish Federations. Prior to his appointment with CJF, he held various Jewish Federation executive positions in New Jersey, Baltimore, Utica, New York, Miami, and Montreal.

*Herman D. Stein* — University Professor and Provost Emeritus, Case Western Reserve University. Former Chairman, Professional Advisory Committee, American Joint Distribution Committee.

*Jonathan Woocher* — Executive Vice-President of the Jewish Education Service of North America (JESNA). Formerly Associate Professor in the

Benjamin S. Hornstein Program in Jewish Communal Service and Director of Continuing Education for Jewish Leadership at Brandeis University.

*Henry L. Zucker* — Director of the Commission on Jewish Education in North America and Consultant to the Mandel Associated Foundations. Served as Executive Director and Executive Vice-President of the Jewish Community Federation of Cleveland from 1948 to 1975.

## STAFF

*Estelle Albeg* — Director, technical support services, Nativ-Policy and Planning Consultants, Jerusalem.

*Mark Gurvis* — Director of Social Planning and Research at the Jewish Community Federation of Cleveland. He is Professional Director of Cleveland's Commission on Jewish Continuity.

*Virginia F. Levi* — Program Director, Premier Industrial Foundation. Previously Staff Associate to the President, Case Western Reserve University, and Associate Director of Admissions, Oberlin College.

*Debbie Meline* — Research and administrative assistant, Nativ-Policy and Planning Consultants, from 1987 to 1990. Coordinator, educational seminars and special projects, the JCC Association, Israel office.

*Joseph Reimer* — Assistant Professor, Hornstein Program in Jewish Communal Service, Brandeis University. Has consulted with several foundations involved in Jewish and general education and done award-winning research in the field of moral development.

## CONSULTANTS

*David Finn* — Chairman of Ruder•Finn, Inc. in New York, New York, one of the largest independent public relations firms in the world. He has long been active in Jewish affairs in North America and for the state of Israel. Author of many books and articles on public affairs, the arts, and business.

*Michael Inbar* — Former Dean of the Faculty of Social Sciences, the Hebrew University of Jerusalem; Professor Emeritus of Cognitive Social Psychology and Education at the Hebrew University, Jerusalem.

*Dena Merriam* — Editorial director and senior writer at Ruder•Finn, Inc. in New York, New York. Author of two books as well as many research reports, articles, corporate newsletters, and a variety of other publications.

## Appendix C:

### Papers Commissioned for the Commission on Jewish Education in North America

*Ackerman, Walter.* "The Structure of Jewish Education in North America," 1990.

A historical perspective on the structure of Jewish education with particular reference to the role of Bureaus of Jewish Education, the religious denominations, and the federation movement.

Professor Ackerman is Shane Family Professor of Education, Ben Gurion University of the Negev.

*Aron, Isa.* "Towards the Professionalization of Jewish Teaching," 1990.

An analysis of the status of Jewish teachers and of the issues involved in the creation of a profession for Jewish teachers.

Dr. Aron is Associate Professor of Jewish Education at the Rhea Hirsch School of Education at Hebrew Union College in Los Angeles.

*Aron, Isa, and Bruce Phillips.* "Findings of the Los Angeles BJE Teacher Census," 1990 (unpublished).

An analysis of the data gathered by the Bureau of Jewish Education of Los Angeles on the teachers in the city's Jewish schools.

Dr. Phillips is Associate Professor of Jewish Communal Service at Hebrew Union College—Jewish Institute of Religion, Los Angeles.

*Davidson, Aryeh.* "The Preparation of Jewish Educators in North America: A Research Study," 1990.

A study of the 14 teacher-training institutions in North America, their student body, faculty, curriculum, and plans for the future.

Professor Davidson is Assistant Professor of Education and Psychology and Head of the Department of Education at the Jewish Theological Seminary of America, New York.

*Fox, Joel.* "Federation-Led Community Planning for Jewish Education, Identity, and Continuity," 1989.

A report on the status and significance of the recently established local commissions on Jewish education/Jewish continuity.

Mr. Fox is Director of Planning and Research at the Jewish Community Federation of Cleveland.

*Gallup* (Israel). "A Pilot Poll of the Jewish Population of the U.S.A.," May 1990 (unpublished).

The Commission participated in a Gallup Omnibus Poll of the Jewish population in North America. The questions related to issues of concern to the Commission on Jewish Education in North America.

*Markovic, Debra and Isa Aron.* "Studies of Personnel in Jewish Education: A Summary Report Prepared for the Commission on Jewish Education in North America," 1990 (unpublished).

A survey of the available data on Jewish educational personnel, their educational background, salary, and benefits.

Ms. Markovic holds a Master's Degree of Education from the University of Judaism in Los Angeles.

*Reimer, Joseph.* "The Synagogue as a Context for Jewish Education," 1990.

A study of how synagogues differ in the ways they support their educational programs and the relationship of a congregational school's receiving favored status and its being a good school.

Professor Reimer is Assistant Professor at the Hornstein Program in Jewish Communal Service, Brandeis University.

*Reisman, Bernard.* "Informal Education in North America" (forthcoming).

A study of the issues involved in informal education in North America with particular reference to the Jewish community centers, the youth movements, camping, family, and adult education.

Professor Reisman is Director of the Hornstein Program in Jewish Communal Service, Brandeis University.

*Scheffler, Israel and Seymour Fox.* "The Relationship between Jewish Education and Jewish Continuity" (forthcoming).

This paper was commissioned in response to questions raised by commissioners concerning the link between Jewish education and Jewish continuity.

Professor Scheffler is Victor S. Thomas Professor of Education and Philosophy at Harvard University.

Professor Fox is Chairman of the Academic Board of the Samuel Mendel Melton Center for Jewish Education in the Diaspora of the Hebrew University, Jerusalem.

*Zucker, Henry L.* "Community Organization for Jewish Education — Leadership, Finance, and Structure," 1989.

An analysis of the role that the organized Jewish community has played in Jewish education as well as a projection of future trends and opportunities.

Mr. Zucker is Director of the Commission on Jewish Education in North America and consultant to the Mandel Associated Foundations.

# APPENDIX D:
## Sources and References

The following sources were used in the preparation of this report:

Aviad, Janet, ed. *Studies in Jewish Education*, vol. 3. Jerusalem: The Magnes Press, 1988.

The Board of Jewish Education of Greater New York. *Jewish Supplementary Schooling: An Educational System in Need of Change.* NY: The Board of Jewish Education, 1988.

Carnegie Forum on Education and the Economy. *A Nation Prepared: Teachers for the 21st Century*, 1986.

Carnegie Foundation for the Advancement of Teaching. *An Imperiled Generation*, 1988.

Chazan, Barry, ed. *Studies in Jewish Education*, vol. 1. Jerusalem: The Magnes Press, 1983.

Cohen, Steven M. "Attitudes of American Jews toward Israel and Israelis: The 1983 National Survey of American Jews and Jewish Communal Leaders." The Institute on American Jewish-Israeli Relations of the American Jewish Committee.

—"Jewish Travel to Israel: Incentives and Inhibitions Among U.S. and Canadian Teenagers and Young Adults." The Jewish Education Committee of the Jewish Agency, 1986.

—"The 1984 National Survey of American Jews: Political and Social Outlooks." The American Jewish Committee, Institute of Human Relations, 1984.

—"Ties and Tensions: The 1986 Survey of American Jewish Attitudes toward Israel and Israelis." The Institute on American Jewish-Israeli Relations of the American Jewish Committee, 1987.

—"Ties and Tensions, an Update: The 1989 Survey of American Jewish Attitudes toward Israel and Israelis." The Institute on American Jewish-Israeli Relations of the American Jewish Committee, 1989.

Davis, Moshe. Memorandum on the university teaching of Jewish civilization, July 1988.

DellaPergola, Sergio and Nitza Genuth. "Jewish Education Attained in Diaspora Communities for 1970s." Research Report Number 2. The Institute of Contemporary Jewry: Hebrew University of Jerusalem, 1983.

Dubb, Allie. "First Census of Jewish Schools in the Diaspora 1981/2-1982/3: Canada." Research Report Number 5. The Institute of Contemporary Jewry: Hebrew University of Jerusalem, 1987.

Dubb, Allie and Sergio DellaPergola. "First Census of Jewish Schools in the Diaspora 1981/2-1982/3: United States of America." Research Report Number 4. The Institute of Contemporary Jewry, Project for Jewish Educational Statistics, and JESNA: Hebrew University of Jerusalem, 1986.

Fishman, Sylvia Barack. *Learning About Learning: Insights on Contemporary Jewish Education from Jewish Population Studies.* Maurice and Marilyn Cohen Center for Modern Jewish Studies: Brandeis University, December 1987.

Fox, Seymour. "Towards a General Theory of Jewish Education." *In The Future of the Jewish Community in North America,* edited by D. Sidorsky. NY: Basic Books, 1973.

Fox, Seymour. "The Vitality of Theory in Schwab's Conception of the Practical." *Curriculum Inquiry* 15:1 (1985).

Genuth, Nitza, Sergio DellaPergola, and Allie Dubb. "First Census of Jewish Schools in the Diaspora 1981/2-1982/3: International Summary." Research Report Number 3. The Institute of Contemporary Jewry: Hebrew University of Jerusalem, 1985.

Goodman, Roberta and Ron Reynolds. "Field Notes." Consultation of 17 Jewish educators, members of CAJE, for the Commission on Jewish Education in North America, 1990.

Himmelfarb, Harold S. and Sergio DellaPergola, eds. *Jewish Education Worldwide: Cross-Cultural Perspectives.* NY: University Press of America, 1989.

Himmelfarb, Milton and David Singer. *American Jewish Yearbook,* vols. 81-86. NY and Philadelphia: American Jewish Committee and the Jewish Publication Society, 1987-88.

Hochstein, Annette. "'The Israel Experience': Educational Programs in Israel." The Jewish Education Committee of the Jewish Agency for Israel, June 1986.

—"Senior Personnel for Jewish Education Progress Report — December 1986." The Jewish Education Committee of the Jewish Agency for Israel, 1986 (unpublished).

The Holmes Group. *Tomorrow's Teachers: A Report of the Holmes Group.* Michigan: The Holmes Group, 1986.

JESNA. "Budgeting and Financing in Jewish Day Schools, 1984."

—"Budgeting and Financing in Jewish Supplementary Schools, 1983."

—"Statistical Highlights of Jewish Schooling in the U.S." Trends 11 (Spring 1986).

JWB. "Directory of Jewish Resident Camps," 1988.

—"Maximizing Jewish Educational Effectiveness of Jewish Community Centers," 1984.

Kosmin, Barry. "Contemporary American Jewry: Implications for Planning." North American Jewish Data Bank, Occasional Paper 4 (June 1988).

Kosmin, Barry, Paul Ritterband, and Jeffrey Scheckner. "Jewish Population in the United States, 1986." *American Jewish Yearbook 1987*, vol. 87. NY: American Jewish Committee & Jewish Publication Society, 1987.

Liebman, Naomi. *Federation Allocations to Jewish Education 1980-84.* NY: CJF Statistics Unit, 1985.

—*Federation Allocations to Jewish Education 1980-86.* NY: CJF Statistics Unit, 1986.

National Commission on Excellence in Education. *Meeting the Challenge of a Nation at Risk.* Cambridge, MA: USA Research, 1984.

—*A Nation at Risk: The Full Account.* Cambridge, MA: USA Research, 1984.

Reimer, Joseph. "The Great Family Debate: Implications for Jewish Education," 1990.

Reimer, Joseph, ed. *To Build a Profession: Careers in Jewish Education.* Waltham, MA: The Hornstein Program in Jewish Communal Service, Brandeis University, 1987.

Rosenak, Michael, ed. *Studies in Jewish Education*, vol. 2. Jerusalem: The Magnes Press, 1984.

Schiff, Alvin I. *Contemporary Jewish Education: Issachar American Style.* NJ: Rossel Books, 1988.

—"Jewish Education at the Crossroads: The State of Jewish Education," 1983. Report prepared for the Joint Program for Jewish Education, in conjunction with CJF, JWB, and JESNA.

Schoem, David. *Ethnic Survival in America: An Ethnography of a Jewish Afternoon School.* Atlanta: Scholars Press, 1989.

—"Explaining Jewish Student Failure." *Anthropology and Education Quarterly* 13:4 (Winter 1982).

Ukeles, Jacob B. "Senior Educator: A Career Option for Jewish Studies Students." The Jewish Education Committee of the Jewish Agency, Publication Number 5, October 1987.

## Appendix E:

### *Consultations and Meetings*

The Commission on Jewish Education in North America held six plenary meetings in New York City:

1. August 1, 1988 – UJA/Federation of Jewish Philanthropies, New York.

2. December 13, 1988 – UJA/Federation of Jewish Philanthropies,New York

3. June 14, 1989 – Hebrew Union College, New York.

4. October 23, 1989 – UJA/Federation of Jewish Philanthropies, New York.

5. February 14, 1990 – UJA/Federation of Jewish Philanthropies, New York.

6. June 12, 1990 – American Jewish Committee, New York.

In addition, the staff of the Commission benefited from the advice of the commissioners and other experts by way of individual and group consultations. The following is a list of those individuals who generously gave of their time to participate in these consultations:

### Individual Consultations

| | | |
|---|---|---|
| Dr. Robert Abramson | — | United Synagogue of America |
| Chaim Botwinick | — | UJA/Federation of Jewish Philanthropies of New York |
| Prof. Steven M. Cohen | — | Queens College of CUNY |
| Prof. David K. Cohen | — | Michigan State University |
| Prof. James Coleman | — | University of Chicago |
| Prof. Lawrence A. Cremin | — | Teachers College of Columbia University |
| Dr. Linda Darling-Hammond | — | Teachers College of Columbia University |
| Prof. Moshe Davis | — | International Center for the University Teaching of Jewish Civilization |
| Mrs. Sylvia Ettenberg | — | Jewish Theological Seminary of America |
| Dr. Paul Flexner | — | JESNA |
| Rabbi Paul Friedman | — | United Synagogue of America |
| Alan Hoffmann | — | The Samuel Mendel Melton Center for Jewish Education in the Diaspora of the Hebrew University, Jerusalem |

| | | |
|---|---|---|
| Dr. Steve Huberman | — | Jewish Federation Council of Greater Los Angeles |
| Dr. Leora Isaacs | — | JESNA |
| Mitchell Jaffe | — | JCC Association |
| Dr. Barry Kosmin | — | North American Jewish Data Bank of the CUNY Graduate Center |
| Prof. H. M. Levin | — | Stanford University |
| Dr. Zeev Mankowitz | — | The Jerusalem Fellows |
| Prof. Daniel Pekarsky | — | University of Wisconsin |
| Arthur Rotman | — | JCC Association |
| Leonard Rubin | — | JCC Association |
| Jeffrey Scheckner | — | CJF |
| Prof. Israel Scheffler | — | Harvard University |
| Prof. Lee S. Shulman | — | Stanford University |
| Prof. Theodore Sizer | — | Brown University |

## GROUP CONSULTATIONS

The following meetings were held in the United States and Israel:

1. September 28, 1988, Jerusalem, Educators' Forum Participants: Walter Ackerman, Barry Chazan, Seymour Fox, Annette Hochstein, Alan Hoffmann, Barry Holtz, Avraham Infeld, Debbie Meline, David Resnick.

2. October 14, 1988, Boston, Research Forum Participants: Jack Bieler, Joshua Elkin, Seymour Fox, Annette Hochstein, Sara Lee, Debbie Meline, Arthur Naparstek, Alvin Schiff, Barry Shrage, Jonathan Woocher.

3. October 27, 1988, Jerusalem, Educators' Forum Participants: Walter Ackerman, Barry Chazan, Seymour Fox, Sol Greenfield, Sam Heilman, Annette Hochstein, Barry Holtz, Avraham Infeld, Jonathan Kestenbaum, Menachem Revivi, David Resnick, Don Scher.

4. March 2, 1989, Brandeis University: Sylvia Fishman, Arthur Naparstek, Joseph Reimer, Susan Shevitz, Larry Sternberg.

5. August 15, 1989, Research Forum, Seattle: Dr. Hanan Alexander, David Ariel, Isa Aron, Aryeh Davidson, Joshua Elkin, Seymour Fox, MarkGurvis, Annette Hochstein, Sara Lee, Alvin Schiff.

6. December 4-5, 1989, CAJE convened the following group of educators for a two-day consultation in Cleveland to consider programmatic areas for the work of the Commission: Harlene Appelman, Ephraim Buchwald, Lynda Cohen, Lavey Darby, Gail Dorph, Marvell Ginsburg, Roberta Goodman, Mark Gurvis, Janet Harris, Charles Herman, Jo Kay, Earl

Lefkovitz, Lenny Matanky, Joseph Reimer, Ron Reynolds, Lifsa Schachter, Eliot Spack, Bobbi Stern, Joy Wasserman, Gary Wexler, Ron Wolfson, Lois Zachary.

7. December 4-5, 1989, Cleveland, Research Forum Participants: Hanan Alexander, Isa Aron, Jack Bieler, Aryeh Davidson, Sharon Feinman-Nemser, Seymour Fox, Annette Hochstein, Alan Hoffmann, Barry Holtz, Michael Inbar, Alvin Schiff, Eliot Spack, Jonathan Woocher.

8. January 25, 1990, New York, Meeting with Orthodox Jewish Educators, convened by Dr. Norman Lamm:Dr. Karen Bacon, Rivkah Behar, Ida Bobrowsky, Joel Boritz, Mrs. Susan Dworken, Rabbi David Eliach, Dr. Ephraim Frankel, Dr. Emanuel Goldman, Rabbi Shraga Gross, Dr. Yitzhak Handel, Rabbi Robert Hirt, David Kolatch, Rabbi Eugene Kwalwasser, Morton L. Mandel, Dr. Leonard Matansky, Dr. Joseph J. Preil, Rabbi Jacob Rabinowitz, Arthur Rotman, Rabbi Martin Schloss, Dr. Mordecai Schnaidman, Audrey Schurgin, Rabbi David G. Shapiro, Dr. Zalman F. Ury, Dr. Harvey Well, Rabbi Yitzhak Witty.

9. January 26, 1990, New York, Meeting with Conservative Movement Jewish Education Cabinet, convened by Dr. Ismar Schorsch: Dr. Robert Abramson, Dr. Hanan Alexander, Dr. Aryeh Davidson, Dr. Sheldon Dorff, Dr. Paul Friedman, Rabbi Hirsch Jacobson, Morton L. Mandel, Dr. Eduardo Rauch, Dr. John Ruskay, Judith Siegel, Dr. Eliot Spiegel, Dr. Jonathan Woocher.

10. February 15, 1990, New York, Meeting with Reform Jewish Educators, convened by Dr. Alfred Gottschalk:Rabbi Howard Bogot, Rabbi Steven Gartin, Mark Gurvis, Sara Lee, Morton L. Mandel, Rabbi Kerry Orlitsky, Dr. Joseph Reimer, Arthur Rotman, Rabbi Jonathan Stein, Zena Sulkus, Jane West, Henry L. Zucker.